DATE DUE

AP 8 '94			
MY 13 '94			
AG 18 '94			
DE 23 '94			
MY 19 '95			
OC 20 '95			
MR 8 '96			
MY 28 97			
MR 5 '98			
NO 5 0			
NO 26 01			

DEMCO 38-296

POWERFUL BUSINESS WRITING

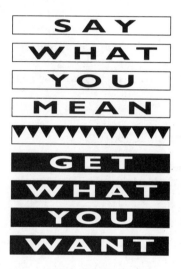

SAY WHAT YOU MEAN

GET WHAT YOU WANT

TOM McKEOWN

Writer's Digest
Cincinnati, Ohio

McGraw-Hill Ryerson
Toronto   Montreal

Published by Writer's Digest Books, an imprint of F&W Publications, Inc., 1507 Dana Avenue, Cincinnati, Ohio 45207. First edition.

96 95 94 93 92   5 4 3 2 1

Library of Congress Cataloguing-in-Publication Data
McKeown, Thomas W.
    Powerful business writing : say what you mean, get what you want /
by Tom McKeown.
        p. c.m.
Rev. ed. of: Write to win. c 1987.
Includes index.
ISBN 0-89879-528-1
1. Business writing.   I. McKeown, Thomas W.   Write to win.
II. Title.
HF5718.3.M36 1992
808'.06665—dc20   91-35721
                                                              CIP

Line illustration page 121 courtesy Harold B. Kirchner, *Wiring Installation and Maintenance* (New York: McGraw-Hill Ryerson Ltd., 1991).

For my Father and Mother

CONTENTS

2 UNDERSTANDING YOUR READER 65

3 ORGANIZING YOUR REPORTS 97

INTRODUCTION

Who Will Benefit from Powerful Business Writing?

You will find *Powerful Business Writing* immediately helpful if your job requires you to write correctly, to present a positive image to the reader, or to organize reports, manuals or essays quickly.

If you are a clerical worker, a supervisor or a manager, you write endless memos, letters and reports. *Powerful Business Writing* provides a systematic way to do this in less time, applying the fundamentals of grammar, tone and organization to all writing tasks.

If you are a university or college student, *Powerful Business Writing* will show you how to express your ideas succinctly, and how to organize your essays effectively. The principles explained here have helped many students to attain first-class marks in their university essays and theses. You can expect similar benefits from your study of this text.

In short, *Powerful Business Writing*'s tips and techniques provide both business and academic benefits.

Specific Benefits

Using *Powerful Business Writing*'s time-tested principles, you can achieve the following specific benefits:

1 Reduce time spent writing by up to 50%
2 Win friends through effective tone
3 Organize reports and essays quickly
4 Increase your confidence by writing correctly
5 Edit work effectively

What Makes Powerful Business Writing Different?

Powerful Business Writing is not a generalized reference text that provides answers to all questions about grammar or tone. Many good books like this exist already—but their size provides the main drawback. The longer they get, the less writers use them.

Powerful Business Writing takes a different approach. It limits information to the minimum necessary to write well. At the same time, it provides sufficient information to present a complete *system* for writing.

In the course of teaching hundreds of university English courses and business writing workshops, I have found that people require better skills in three key areas: Grammar, Psychology of Communication and Organization. This handbook answers these needs. I have included only information essential for most business and academic writers.

To summarize, you may not know *everything* when you finish this book, but you will know everything *necessary* to communicate well.

How to Use the Book

You can use *Powerful Business Writing* to supplement courses in Business Writing, Adult Basic Education, English grammar or English as a Second Language. You can also use it as a self-paced correspondence writing program. If you are a graduate of *Written Power* or other business writing workshops, you can use this book to refresh and update your understanding.

Powerful Business Writing contains sample exercises to allow you to check your level of understanding. Answer Keys are provided at the end of each of the book's three major sections: Writing Clearly, Understanding Your Reader and Organizing Your Reports.

A Special Thanks

A special thanks to those who assisted with this book. In particular, I'm grateful to my students and to graduates of *Written Power*, who have helped refine the techniques presented here by their criticism and advice. Also, special thanks to my wife, Rosalind, to William Messenger, and to David Quinlivan-Hall for their friendly, careful and useful criticism.

1 *WRITING CLEARLY*

OBJECTIVES:

- Recognize Subject- and Object-Nouns

- Recognize Linking and Action Verbs

- Recognize the Active and Passive Voice

- Use Specific Words

- Write Power Sentences

- Build Unified, Coherent Paragraphs

- Use Transitional Markers Effectively

INTRODUCTION

To write simply is as difficult as to be good.
—W. Somerset Maugham

Clarity comes *first* in good business writing. You may think of good ideas, but until you capture them clearly on paper you cannot communicate them to other people.

Translating abstract thoughts into clear, concrete words takes practice. Some people may seem to you to write clearly without effort. At the same time, you may think that you have to spend more time revising for clarity than other people in the office. Don't be misled. All clear writing requires hard work. Of course, others may have studied far longer than you, or taken to writing more easily.

This section will unlock the powerful techniques all good writers use to communicate, and put them to work for *you.* Having learned these key techniques, you will communicate your written ideas to others more quickly and effectively.

Basically, to write well you will need to learn how to write a clear sentence and a logically constructed paragraph. In order to write clear sentences you will need to learn, or re-learn, the following terms:

1 Noun (Subject and Object nouns)
2 Verb (Action and Linking verbs)
3 The Active Voice
4 The Passive Voice (Regular and Divine)

If you dislike grammar, learning these terms may give you a headache. That's the bad news. The good news is that once you learn *first* how to distinguish them, and *second* how to apply them, you will be well on your way to writing crisp memos and clear letters.

If you want to overcome your dread of

grammar once and for all, pour yourself a cup
of coffee, unplug the phone, and settle in for a
solid learning session.

I THE SENTENCE

The *single* sentence represents the hammer in the writer's tool kit. The sentence conveys a single unit of thought, and this function is critically important. No matter how long your letters or reports, they consist of individual sentences that your reader encounters one at a time. The quality of these sentences determines the overall quality of your writing. Before going on to define the inner qualities and form that turn an ordinary sentence into what I term the *power sentence*, let's discuss the simpler question of length.

SENTENCE LENGTH

In practice, sentences can run anywhere from two words ("Jim succeeded.") to hundreds (think of typical legal agreements). In general, your sentences should *average* no more than fifteen words, with some using as few as two words, and others as many as thirty. Why use so few words in business writing? Because that's all most readers can absorb quickly. Yet sentences in many modern business letters often average twenty-five words or more—far too many. Learn to compress your ideas.

THE READER'S VIEWPOINT

Let's examine how a sentence works from the reader's viewpoint, so that you can understand why you should limit the length of your sentences.

You may know that the period at the end of a sentence signals the end of a complete thought. But what activity does the *reader* engage in when he or she encounters a period? The reader does not simply put the mind in neutral gear at this time, but actively *thinks about* the meaning of the sentence just concluded, and its connection to previous thoughts.

The reader does not simply *digest* the meaning of the sentence—he or she may prefer to leave it undigested. For example, you will not simply *absorb* the meaning of this sentence when you come to its period, you will think about it, perhaps *judge* it. If you disagree with the content of what I say, you may let it slide out of your mind; if the form of my sentence confuses you, you may stop trying to understand my message.

Your readers respond in the same way. They may tune you out if you convey your message in sentences too long to follow easily. Busy readers find it bothersome to hold a lengthy sentence in their memory long enough to accept or reject it. They prefer fairly short sentences, which permit quick identification of the main action and the main meaning. In literary writing, sentences are often much longer and more complex because their intention is to move the reader to reflection, rather than action. Other differences between business and literary English appear in point form on the opposite page. Don't make the mistake of following literary models. Remember that, in business writing, "Small is beautiful."

Table Showing Differences between Literary and Business English

Literary Writing	Business Writing
Designed to be read many times	Reveals full meaning on a single reading
Complex expression	Clear expression
Unfamiliar words	Familiar words
Colorful tone	Plain language
Variety expected	Consistency expected
Imagery and symbolism	Numbers and charts
Long, complex sentences	Short, clear sentences
Impossible to read quickly	Can be read quickly
Ambiguity acceptable	Clarity essential
Leads reader to REFLECT	Leads reader to ACT

Notes:

1. Most people have been trained by English teachers of a literary leaning: hence the stubborn reluctance to abandon creative writing in the office on the part of some "well-educated" business writers.

2. Even when literary sentences are clear, as in Hemingway's novels, the themes require lengthy reflection.

3. When literary works enforce a specific interpretation they veer towards propaganda, as in George Orwell's *1984*. True literature has no design on the reader, other than to promote a sense of interconnectedness between individuals of different societies and ages through increased self-understanding, tolerance and sensitivity to nuance.

WHY DO PEOPLE WRITE LONG SENTENCES?

Because they haven't the ability to write short ones!

Most readers find letters with an average sentence length of only fourteen words easily comprehensible. Aim for a good mix of short and longer sentences, however, to provide variety and keep the reader alert. Also, express difficult thoughts in short sentences, and easier thoughts in longer sentences. When your readers are required to expend only a small amount of their mental energy to decipher the *form* of your sentence, they have more energy to comprehend your *meaning*.

HOW MANY MAIN IDEAS SHOULD I PACK INTO A SENTENCE?

It takes less time to learn to write nobly than to learn to write lightly and straight- forwardly.
—F.W. Nietzsche

As a rough guide, aim to write sentences that convey only *one main idea* (simple or complex sentences) about eighty per cent of the time. That leaves fifteen per cent of your sentences to convey two main ideas at once (compound sentences), and five per cent of your sentences to convey three ideas or more. These "three-idea" sentences often appear in the form of a list, which readers can follow very easily.

Since eighty per cent of your sentences should convey only one main idea, you can see that writing them represents your most critical writing task. Let's look at how to write these "one-main-idea" sentences so as to maximize their precision of thought and impact on the reader. I call the perfectly written "one-main- idea" sentence the *power sentence.*

II *THE POWER SENTENCE*

The *power sentence* presents one main thought, uses the active voice, uses an action verb and uses specific words. It can be summarized in the form of this checklist:

Three-Step Checklist for Writing a Power Sentence

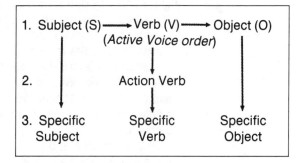

1. Subject (S) ——► Verb (V) ——► Object (O)
   (*Active Voice order*)

2. Action Verb

3. Specific   Specific   Specific
   Subject   Verb   Object

That is, the *power sentence*:

1 Uses the active voice (S —► V —►O order)
2 Uses an action verb (not a linking verb)
3 Uses specific words (not generalized ones).

Once you understand and can implement these qualities, you will have a stranglehold on grammar. Also, your sentences will clearly communicate your intended meaning. In order to learn the meaning of these concepts, you'll have to begin by mastering a number of definitions. First, we'll define nouns and verbs. Next, we'll arrange them within the sentence to form the active voice. After that, we'll show you how to recognize the passive voice—in order to avoid it. Then we'll learn how to choose specific words. Finally, you'll complete a review exercise to see how much you've learned, and how much still needs some improvement. After mastering *power sentences*, we can turn our attention to assembling them into *power paragraphs*.

A

RECOGNIZING NOUNS

A noun is a word used to name a person, a place or a thing; it comes from the Latin word *nomen*, which means "name." The following words are all nouns: *map, territory, procedure, initiation, Williams Lake, vice-president, Kate.*

Two slightly different types of words are also classified as nouns, and act in the same way: pronouns and noun phrases. Pronouns are words that, as the meaning of the Latin prefix *pro* suggests, stand *for* nouns in a sentence: *she, he, it, they.* Noun phrases are groups of two or more words that together identify a single person or thing: *The Director of Corrections.*

Both pronouns and noun phrases perform the same function as nouns: they identify the *doers* and the *receivers* of actions in a sentence: *She* [pronoun identifying the "doer"] influences *department policy* [noun phrase identifying the "receiver"]. Depending on its function in a particular sentence, a noun, pronoun or noun phrase may act as either a *doer*, a "subject," or *receiver*, an "object." To write power sentences you must be able to distinguish subject-nouns from object-nouns, so we will now explain how to make this distinction.

SUBJECT-NOUNS

Nouns within a sentence function in different ways, and take on different names with different functions. The word "subject-noun," for example, has a special meaning in grammar. It does not refer to the noun expressing the topic of the sentence, or what the sentence is about. Instead, it refers to the noun which *performs the action* described by the verb in the sentence: "The *manager* approved my report." Here the "manager" approved, and this noun ("manager") represents the subject of the sentence.

OBJECT-NOUNS

"Object-noun" refers to the noun which receives the action performed by the subject-noun: "The manager approved my *report*." Here the object-noun ("report") receives the action "approved." As a general rule, the "receiver" of the action (the object) should come *after* the verb in the sentence. Notice that you *can* place the object in front of the verb: "My *report* was approved by the manager." However, power sentences avoid this pattern since it leads to the undesirable passive voice structure, which we will examine more closely later.

EXERCISE 1

Circle the subject-nouns, and underline the object-nouns, in the following sentences. Remember that the subject-noun *performs* the *action* in the sentence, and that some of the sentences are tricky.

1 The memo set forth seven purchase options.

2 After several years of neglect, he organized his budget.

3 My letter was cut in half by the hard-nosed editor.

4 Bill conducted tests on the three-blade propeller.

5 The analysis of results was presented by the field engineer.

6 The financial statements for Stetson Inc. were analyzed by the accountants.

7 We will sell our subsidiary companies in two years.

8 Mr. White's report contained several errors.

9 The company fired all of its employees.

10 George Marvin received a pay increase after he had worked for 15 years.

11 A new personnel manager has been hired by the company.

12 The vice-president asked me to handle the Chadwick account.

13 The new director of programming started his career as a radio announcer.

14 Before we can rent this car, we must make sure it is insured.

15 Several programs were run by Joanne at the seminar.

Recognizing Subject- and Object-Nouns

Check your answers with the answer key on page 55. Review the preceding definitions if your answers are not correct. If you scored 100%, pat yourself on the back!

B *RECOGNIZING VERBS*

Now that you have been briefly introduced to the two main classes of nouns, subjects and objects, you are ready to classify verbs in the same way. Verbs divide into two categories: *action verbs* and *linking verbs.* Power sentences use action verbs rather than linking verbs, so we will now define each type.

LINKING VERBS

The most common linking verb is some form of the verb "to be":

- Sharon *is* an above-average worker.
- The hot tub samples *are* contaminated.
- The department *is* of medium size.
- The managers *are* well qualified.
- The complaint *was* valid.
- The officials *were* forward-looking.
- The report *will be* several pages long.

Notice that the linking verb can occur in any tense: past (*was, were*); present (*is, are*); or future (*will be*).

Most people find it easier to write with linking verbs than action verbs, but this style weakens the impact of your writing. Linking verbs link the subject of a sentence with the noun or adjective that follows: Harry *is* a driver. Notice that words "Harry" and "driver" represent the same person; the sentence links complementary ideas together, and therefore contains a relatively small amount of information, compared to one using an action verb.

ACTION VERBS

Action verbs, unlike linking verbs, express an action of the body (*clamber, waddle, slide*) or the mind (*deny, judge, approve*). For this reason, they energize writing. The action verb tells your reader what the subject-noun *does*:

- Susan *rewrote* the report.
- Barry *distributed* the affidavits.
- Ho-lee *evaluated* the computer software.
- The guard *slumbered.*

CHANGING LINKING TO ACTION VERBS

To replace a linking verb with an action verb, you need to rethink what you want to tell your reader. For example, the sentence we looked at earlier, "Harry *is* a driver" can be rewritten as "Harry *drives* an MGB." Similarly, "Sharon *is* a student of psychology" can be recast as "Sharon *studies* psychology." This sentence conveys more information and mental energy, in fewer words, than the linking verb version does. It brings two distinct ideas, Sharon and psychology, into a dynamic rather than a static relationship. In mathematical terms, you might think of a linking verb as a plus sign (+), adding together two complementary ideas ("I *am* Tarzan"), and an action verb as a multiplication ("×") sign, powerfully transmitting energy between two *different* entities ("Tarzan *fights* crocodiles"). Action verbs express thought more powerfully than linking verbs.

As another example, we can change the sentence "He *is* [linking verb] inclined to disagree with his manager" to "He often *disagrees* [action verb] with his manager." Similarly, "Her budget presentation *will be* [linking verb] half an hour in length" becomes "Her budget presentation *will require* [action verb] half an hour."

EXERCISE 2   Circle the linking verbs. Rewrite the sentences, replacing the linking verbs with action verbs. Notice that you may need to change the order of the nouns in some sentences to use an action verb.

1 The second memo is sixteen pages longer than the first one.

2 The president and the executive committee are in agreement.

3 The lieutenant will be an effective leader of the men.

4 Jim was pleased with the children's development.

5 This layout will be satisfactory to the staff.

6 With a word processor, you are free to shift text around.

7 The chief executive officer is quick to adopt new methods.

8 Janice is an efficient computer programmer.

9 Alex is responsible for investigating all accidents that occur on company premises.

10 A comprehensive management training program is useful for all employees.

11 The assessment team was in a meeting at the Pacific Hotel.

12 Each employee is ready for work by 9 a.m.

---

13 Alice was well qualified for the position of credit manager.

---

14 The air is cold and wet.

---

15 The courier was late bringing the new contracts.

Changing Linking Verbs to Action Verbs

Check your answers with the answer key on page 56. This ability to change linking to action verbs poses the greatest challenge to most writers. So far so good?

C *THE ACTIVE VOICE*

Now that you can identify the subject, object and action verb, you are ready to place them in the most powerful sentence order: Subject—Action Verb—Object.

This order identifies the *active voice*. All you have learned to this point has equipped you to write sentences in this active voice pattern. Purpose? To ensure the clearest expression of your thinking.

Before going further, be particularly careful not to confuse the terms "action verb" and "active voice." As explained above, we call words that express actions "action verbs." On the other hand, the term "active voice" refers to sentences that follow the subject-noun, action verb, object-noun pattern (S—V—O). This is the opposite of the passive structure (O—V—S).

THE REGULAR ACTIVE (S—V—O)

To take the first step in writing an active voice sentence, ensure that the subject-noun comes in front of the action verb. Do you know how to locate the subject-noun of your sentences in order to put it before your verb? Take this passive voice sentence for example: "The chairman was elected by the committee." Follow the three steps in this checklist:

Table: How to Locate the Subject-Noun

> 1 Locate the action verb, and put it in the present tense. ("elect")
>
> 2 Give this verb an "*ing*" ending. ("electing")
>
> 3 Ask, "Who or what *does* the [*verb*]ing?" (the committee)
>
> * The answer to question number 3 *always* provides the grammatical "subject" of your sentence.

Then, simply place the subject-noun before the verb in your sentence. ("*The committee* elected the chairman.")

Now try the same with this passive voice sentence: "The question was answered by the manager."

To find the subject:

1 Simplify the verb phrase "was answered" (which is in the past tense) to the present tense, "*answer*";
2 Give the verb an "ing" ending, "answer*ing*";
3 Ask, "Who or what *does* the answering?"

Obviously, the *manager* does the "answering," and is therefore the true "subject" of the sentence. Therefore, you rewrite the sentence to place it first: "*The manager* answered the question."

EXERCISE 3   Using the three-step procedure outlined above, circle the grammatical subject in each of these sentences; then rewrite each sentence, if necessary, in the active voice pattern. Check your answer with the answer key, page 58.

1 The public information officer was misled by the letter.

2 The field staff were delighted by the supervisor's appointment.

3 Bill engineered the satellite tracking antenna.

4 "Why bother?" drawled Sleepy.

5 A copy of the report is sent by the client.

6 Disciplinary action is taken by the supervisor after thoroughly investigating the incident.

7 Administrative staff are authorized by the company to ensure that employees conform to the company's dress code.

8 Two probationary reviews are written by the manager for each employee.

9 Andrea was dismayed by Mr. Aiken's poor reaction to her presentation.

10 You will be presented with a free sample from our company.

11 New employees will be advised by the department head regarding the location of their lockers.

12 Six employees were honored with a long service recognition ceremony.

13 A trip to Japan was received by Joe Morgan for his outstanding sales record last year.

Rewriting in the Active Voice

14 All overtime hours must be confirmed by the employee's department head.

Writing sentences in the active voice (S—V—O) will give your letters more punch, impact and clarity than any other possible improvement. So . . . practice, practice, practice.

THE SPECIAL ACTIVE VOICE PATTERN (V—O)

One kind of sentence may confuse you when attempting to write in the active voice. What is the subject here, for example?: "Please send a copy of the report to Mr. Lum." The verb is "send," but who or what does the sending? The answer is the person for whom the sentence is intended ("[*You*] please send a copy of the report to Mr. Lum").

The subject in this kind of sentence is understood as "You." The reader instinctively knows that a sentence which begins with a verb has "you" for its subject. Although the subject is not named, it is clear, and obviously comes before the verb. Therefore this Verb—Object sentence pattern follows the active voice pattern, just as though the subject were present. Be careful not to confuse it with the Verb—Subject (V—S) sentence pattern,

however, which marks the notorious divine
passive pattern (about which, more later).

SUMMARY

*The
grammarians
are at
variance, and
the matter is
still undecided.*
—Horace

At this point, you have learned how to identify
the subjects, objects and verbs in your
sentences, in order to write in the active voice.
You have also learned the correct order in
which to place them. In order to edit your own
writing, you also need to be able to recognize
the passive voice when it occurs. Just as the
active voice marks the professional writer, so
the passive voice characterizes the
bureaucratic, foggy-minded buck-passer.

THE PASSIVE VOICE

Two forms of the passive voice sentence lurk
in the woods of the writer's mind: the *regular
passive* and the *divine passive*. We'll examine
each in some detail, in order to keep them out
of our way.

THE REGULAR PASSIVE (O—V—S)

The regular passive sentence follows this word
order: O—V—S. For example, in the sentence
"Ariel was promoted by Frank," the noun
"Ariel" receives the action initiated by "Frank."
Therefore, "Ariel" is the object-noun. Since
this word precedes the verb, the sentence
follows the O—V—S (regular passive) pattern.

The passive pattern drains energy from your
sentences. Rewrite the sentence to read,
"Frank promoted Ariel." Notice that this (active
voice) sentence requires only three words,
whereas the passive voice sentence requires
five words to say the same thing.

Why Do Intelligent People often Write in the Passive Voice?

Many relatively intelligent and sophisticated thinkers use the passive voice far too often. Why? The answer may be that although we *think* in the active voice (Frank promoted Ariel), when we come to *write* our thoughts, we recall the last word that we actually thought (Ariel) first; then we recall the verb (was promoted by); finally, we recall the subject (Frank). This causes us to write "backwards," in the passive voice (Ariel was promoted by Frank).

Imagine watching a home movie of someone walking out of the house, then diving into the swimming pool—being run backwards. It's funny at first, then annoying. Take the time to rewind the film, then run it forward. If you express yourself in the active voice your readers will register your ideas more easily and quickly.

The greater part of this world's troubles are due to questions of grammar.
—Montaigne

You will most likely fall into the passive voice sequence when dealing with complex thoughts, rather than with simple actions: "The impeachment (object) was conducted (verb) after many delays and a great deal of argument by the Senate committee" (subject). Therefore, exercise particular caution with your sentence structure when formulating sophisticated concepts—such as legal agreements. Lawyers, take note!

THE DIVINE PASSIVE (O—V)

Both the active voice and the regular passive voice sentences contain a subject noun, either before or after the verb. Sometimes, however, a sentence contains no subject at all. This form of sentence follows the *divine passive* structure (O—V). Take this sentence, for example: "The specimens were analyzed." Since the writer provides no subject (which performs the action described by the verb) the reader can only assume that an unseen person or force must have performed the analysis.

The Chief Drawback of the Divine Passive

The qualifier "divine" in the phrase "divine passive" ironically implies that the actor in the sentence must be in the heavens or sitting on a cloud somewhere! Writers often resort to this form when they want to dodge responsibility for an action through anonymity.

For example, they might write "Your application for vacation leave has not been approved." Does this mean that no manager in the company denied your application? Or, "A decision has been made not to ratify your nomination for the position." Does this mean no influential person opposed your nomination? Or, "Another person has been selected for the position." Does this mean the person signing the letter to you did not have a hand in, or support, the decision? Of course this might be the case; nevertheless, the reader will very likely draw the opposite conclusion (whether correct or not!). Therefore, such grammatical refuges—or subterfuges— are pointlessly evasive. The reader will always assume that the person who signed the letter has taken the action, or supports it.

Let's look at another example: "Your lease has been cancelled." Cancelled by whom? Why? Struggling with the disquieting fact that an anonymous authority is directing a negative power in your direction, you may want to know which person to challenge, or in which direction to assert your own power.

On the other hand, providing your reader with a clear subject in sentences signals your willingness to accept responsibility: for example, "*We* have cancelled your lease because of non-payment of dues," or "Since *you* have not paid your dues, *your* lease has lapsed."

I have often wished that there were a language in which it would be impossible to tell a lie.
—G.C. Lichtenberg

Turning the Divine Passive Active

But how do you turn a tricky phrase like the following one from the divine passive into the active voice?: *Your application for vacation leave has been denied.* First, you have to notice that the subject is missing—then, provide one. Remembering your three-step "How to Find the Subject-Noun" checklist, you would follow these steps:

1 Find the verb phrase: "has been denied"
2 Add "ing" to the verb: "deny-ing"
3 Ask, "Who or what does the denying?"

The vacation leave does not deny itself, so it can't be the subject. The subject is missing. The reader must guess who performed the action, and this causes unnecessary confusion. For example: "The personnel manager denied your application for vacation leave."

If you can't provide a subject, you may have nothing to say—in which case delete the sentence—or you may not have thought clearly—in which case stop and think! Then rewrite.

Should the Divine Passive Ever Be Used?

Yes. You can effectively use the divine passive to convey *welcome* news: "Your application has been accepted."; "You have been elected to the board."; "Your film has been nominated for an award." Here your anonymity will be seen as the mark of modesty rather than cowardice.

The divine passive is also sometimes appropriate when the subject-noun is irrelevant or unknown—that is, where you are obviously not attempting to avoid responsibility for an action: "My purse was stolen on the bus." However, even here you could effectively write, "*Someone* on the bus stole my purse."

With these two exceptions, however, strive to kick the vast majority of your sentences out of the mental hammock which the passive voice provides.

EXERCISE 4   Circle the grammatical subject-nouns of the
following sentences, where present. Underline
the objects. Double-underline the verbs.
Provide a subject-noun if needed, and rewrite
all the sentences in subject—verb—object
order, using action verbs.

   1 Labor peace has been sought.

   2 A way will be found to master this material.

   3 Susan is considered a successful
     negotiator.

   4 One was struck by the clock.

   5 The moon was jumped over by the cow.

   6 Sam weighed the alternatives and made a
     decision.

   7 Grievances are handled in accordance with
     the step approach method.

   8 Every effort will be made to handle
     problems as they arise.

   9 The safety rules are designed to ensure
     employees avoid accidents.

  10 Employees are advised by management not
     to bring excessive amounts of money or
     valuables to the workplace.

  11 Vacation times are allocated in accordance
     with each employee's years of service to
     the company.

12 There is nothing to be done about our high absentee rate.

13 You were asked to submit the report no later than 3 p.m. on Tuesday, December 22.

14 Sick leave is payable only when a regular full- or part-time employee is absent from work as a result of an illness or non-work related injury.

15 Requests for credit information regarding company employees are received in writing.

Changing the Passive to the Active Voice

Check your versions against the answer key on page 60. If you scored 100%, you have a good grasp of the active voice (and a significant element of English grammar!)

E *BEING SPECIFIC*

Once you know how to use the active voice (S—V—O order), and action verbs, you have accomplished two-thirds of the journey toward writing effective sentences. The final one-third involves *being specific.* When you add this quality of specificity to the active voice and the use of action verbs, you will have attained the ability to write the *power sentence.*

RECOGNIZING UMBRELLA VERBS

Check your sentences for specific words, beginning with your choice of verb. For example, in the sentence "The manager handles reports," the action verb "handles" does not convey a clear picture. It could mean "reviews," "approves," "shreds," "burns," "drafts," "writes," or many other specific activities.

Generalized verbs like "handles" are "umbrella words," under which huddle multitudes of specific meanings. In using these vague words, the writer is saying to the reader, "Guess what I mean!" The bewildered reader irritably concludes that such writers either do not know what they mean themselves, cannot be bothered to be clear, or intend to conceal their meaning from their readers. Not the best approach! Much better to peer under the umbrella and select the most appropriate specific word from those sheltering there.

RECOGNIZING UMBRELLA NOUNS

The same advice applies to your choice of subject- and object-nouns: look under the umbrella for the specific word. Instead of saying "the report," say "the quarterly report"; instead of the "appropriate authorities" say "the selection committee." By taking the trouble to locate the specific word for the exact meaning you wish to convey, you will save your reader time and energy.

F THE POWER SENTENCE: SUMMARY AND REVIEW

Putting all these bits of advice together, let's see how they would affect your attitude to a sentence you might have written like this one, "The report was handled by the executive member."

The *power sentence* checklist given earlier will show you how to edit this sentence in three steps. Here it is again:

**Three-Step
Checklist for
Writing a
Power
Sentence**

1 Put sentence in Subject—Verb—Object
  order.
2 Make sure the verb is an Action Verb.
3 Make sure your Subject, Verb and
  Object are specific.

Checking the example given above against
this list, you would notice that it displays three
shortcomings: the passive voice order (O—V—
S); a vague, umbrella verb; and general,
umbrella nouns (both subject and object). You
would therefore improve it in three stages:

S   V   O

S—V—O   1 The executive member handled the report.

Action Verb   2 The executive member *approved* the report.

Specifics   3 Our *vice-president* approved my *1989
budget forecast.*

Your own revision might differ in your choice of
specific words, but your changes would help
your reader by providing clarity and concision.

EXERCISE 5 Turn this passive voice sentence into a power
sentence:
"*The course was talked about by the people
concerned.*"
  Notice that the subject, verb and object are
all umbrella words. You will have to provide
specific replacements to rewrite the sentence
successfully.

1 _____.

S   V   O

2 _____.

action verb

3 _____.

specific subject specific verb specific object

**Writing the
Power
Sentence**

Check your answers on page 62. Notice that the *Power Sentence Checklist* keeps you from waffling, and ensures that you have something specific to tell your reader.

If you can now recognize and write power sentences, congratulations! You've mastered more English technique than many students— and some teachers—ever will.

G *PUNCTUATION*

Punctuation marks divide—or link—ideas. Remember that you use punctuation to help increase your reader's understanding of what you have written. If you do not use correct punctuation, your readers may well misinterpret your meaning. For example, notice how a lack of punctuation distorts the meaning of the following sentence:

> Your order for the continuous feed printer paper and software has been delayed.

Without punctuation, this sentence could refer to only two items: paper used for a continuous feed printer and software. However, the original order actually specified three items; therefore, the sentence should read:

> Your order for the continuous feed printer, paper and software has been delayed.

To understand correct business punctuation, you need to examine the four most useful punctuation marks: the comma, the semi-colon, the colon and the dash.

Comma

**First Use of
the Comma**

The comma has four main uses.

Put a comma after a word or phrase which begins a sentence and comes before the words which express the main idea. The comma could follow a single word or a whole phrase. Single words followed by commas include: "however," "nevertheless," "first" or "sometimes." For example:

> However, we should not use this product in our company.

*Commas are
used when you
have to take a
breath, and
periods are
used when you
want to stop
and think.*
—Anon

Phrases which introduce a sentence often begin with words such as "if," "when," "while," "after," etc. For example:

> While I was eating, the sales manager telephoned my client.

If you did not place a comma after "eating," the meaning of this sentence would be comically obscured: "While I was eating the sales manager telephoned my client." You wouldn't want to imply that you made a practice of eating the sales manager!

Here's another example of an introductory phrase followed by a comma:

> After the vice-president circulated the report on time-management techniques, office efficiency improved.

Commas which follow an introductory phrase in a sentence help the readers to distinguish the introductory phrase from the main thought and so avoid confusion.

**Second Use
of the Comma**

Use commas to set off an *interrupting construction* within a sentence, or, for a slightly different effect, use parentheses or dashes. To understand this second use of the comma, you need to first define the term interrupting construction.

Grammarians define an interrupting construction as a group of words inside a sentence which can be removed without changing the meaning of the rest of the sentence. That is, the remaining words contain a subject and a verb, and express a complete thought, regardless of the information in the interrupting construction. For example:

> The annual meeting, which all staff members must attend, will take place on October 23.

Notice that the phrase "which all staff members must attend" acts as an interrupting construction; the sentence could stand without it and still be correct:

> The annual meeting will take place on October 23.

The interrupting construction merely adds extra information to clarify the importance of the meeting.

You can also use *dashes, parentheses* or *square brackets* to set off an interrupting construction within a sentence.

The Dash

Use dashes to highlight the interrupting information by accentuating it. This use of the dash makes the interrupting construction more important than the rest of the sentence. For example:

> All clients—even those opposed to our philosophy—must be treated with respect.

You may also use dashes for other reasons that will be covered in the section on the dash below.

Parentheses

Use parentheses to make the interrupting construction something like a whisper—that is, less important than the rest of the sentence and more like an aside. For example:

Credit Unions (sometimes mistaken for Savings & Loan Associations) serve the needs of a particular company.

Square Brackets

Use square brackets to enclose editorial interruptions in a quotation. For example, if you were writing an article quoting someone who misspelled a person's name, you would spell the name correctly inside the square brackets immediately following the misspelled version. For example:

Dr. Brackendale pointed out in her speech: "Mr. Bunion's [Onion's] proposal has several layers to it."

You also use square brackets when you quote from someone else's writing and must insert a word to make the meaning clearer. For example:

Mr. Smith's report stated: "The [industrial] community must seriously consider re-cycling its waste materials."

Third Use of the Comma

Use a comma to introduce an informal quotation. For example:

He then asked me if I had received the June receipts that morning. I remember my reply exactly. I said, "Yes, they came in at 11:05."

Note that an informal quotation usually reports what someone has *said* in conversation. When you write the quotation, "Yes, they came in at 11:05.", you must capitalize the first letter of yes because it is the first word in the quotation, even though it was preceded by a comma.

When you use *quotation marks*, remember to use *double quotation marks* to identify the beginning and end of a word-for-word quotation and to use *single quotation marks* to indicate a paraphrase or a quotation within a quotation. For example: "Ms. Smith said, 'Yes, they came in at 11:05.' "

Fourth Use of the Comma

Use a comma between two independent clauses joined by a coordinating conjunction if the subject changes in the second clause. For example:

> He was going to enter the code, but the manager had switched off the override toggle.

In this sentence, "he" is the subject of the first independent clause, while "the manager" is the subject of the second independent clause. Because these two clauses begin with different subjects and are joined by the coordinating conjunction "but," a comma must be inserted.

Note that there are only seven coordinating conjunctions: *and, but, or, nor, for, yet* and *so*. Here are some more examples:

> The secretary organized the travel arrangements, and the sales manager contacted the conference facilitator.

> Elsa enjoys working with numbers, but George prefers customer relations.

Semi-Colon

The semi-colon functions mainly to separate two ideas within the same sentence. Of course, you could ask why not just use a period instead of a semi-colon and make two sentences? You use a semi-colon instead of a period in cases where you want to indicate that one action caused another, or both actions occurred at the same time, or the two actions relate closely in some other way. To show such a relationship, you can use the semi-colon in two ways.

First Use of the Semi-Colon

Use a semi-colon to join two independent clauses that are not joined by a coordinating conjunction. Remember the seven coordinating conjunctions: *and, but, so, for, nor, or* and *yet*. Here is a sentence incorrectly punctuated with a comma because it contains no coordinating conjunction and joins two independent clauses:

> The collections officer opposed the request, the customer relations supervisor approved it.

The two halves of this sentence cannot be joined by a comma because a comma lacks sufficient strength. To punctuate this sentence correctly, place a semi-colon between the two parts of the sentence:

> The collections officer opposed the request; the customer relations supervisor approved it.

Second Use of the Semi-Colon

Use a semi-colon between independent clauses joined by a conjunctive adverb. A conjunctive adverb is a word which describes the nature of the relationship between two independent clauses. You may use words such as *accordingly, however, consequently, therefore, subsequently, nonetheless, moreover, instead* and *furthermore* as conjunctive adverbs in a sentence. For example:

> The vice-president interceded on behalf of Ajax Supplies; however, the company decided to use a different supplier.

When you use a semi-colon followed by a conjunctive adverb such as "however," you must place a comma after the word "however." Here is another example:

> The personnel manager neglected his duties; consequently, we must hire a new personnel manager.

The Colon

In general, you use the colon to direct your reader's attention forward. A colon usually occurs near the beginning of a sentence and indicates that something çhallenging, interesting or difficult approaches: a list, a complex quotation, a formal statement. You can use the colon in three ways.

First Use of the Colon

Use a colon to introduce a long, formal quotation. For example:

> The *accounts manual* defines an Interest Achiever Account as follows: "The IAA is an account in which interest is paid at increasingly higher rates depending on the daily closing balance."

Second Use of the Colon

Use a colon to introduce a list. For example:

> Interest rates for these increments are as follows: 9.35%, 9.46%, 10.60%, and 11.43%.

Third Use of the Colon

Use a colon after phrases which include "the following" and "as follows." For example:

> We should proceed with the takeover as follows: appoint an accounts manager, evaluate our financial status, and study alternate locations.

The Dash

You have already read how to use two dashes to set off an interrupting construction. You can also use one dash to direct the reader's attention backwards—unlike the colon, which directs the reader's attention forward. Usually, therefore, the dash occurs towards the end of a sentence and requires the reader to backtrack in order to fully comprehend the sentence's meaning. For example:

> The proposal to amend flex time had one marked effect—it upset all the staff.

In this example, the words following the dash emphasize or comment on the preceding idea. Here's another example:

> Careful and correct punctuation provides your sentence with one important feature—clarity of thought.

Note that you should not confuse the dash with the hyphen. You use two strokes of the hyphen key to type a dash. Use the hyphen as a mark of internal word division, as in the word "sub-contractor."

EXERCISE 6

Apply the rules of punctuation specified above to punctuate the following sentences correctly. Check your answers on page 62.

Punctuation

1 As soon as I arrived I corrected the punctuation in my letter.

2 The personnel manager will advertise the position the vice-president will conduct the interviews.

3 Meet us on the fifth floor not the fourth floor in three hours.

4 The client thanked Ms. Martin Marten for her excellent report.

5 Secondly I would like to discuss how my proposal will increase profits.

SUMMARY
If you can now use these four punctuation marks correctly, you are ready to progress from writing power sentences to writing power paragraphs.

III THE POWER PARAGRAPH

Just as a sentence describes a *transfer of energy* from a subject-noun to an object-noun, a paragraph links sentences together into a *sequence of combined energies* having a central core of meaning. The word "paragraph" comes from the Greek *para*, meaning beside, plus *graphos*, meaning mark. Originally the word referred to a short stroke placed within the tightly crabbed script of a papyrus manuscript to mark the beginning of a new thought.

Now that paper is less expensive, we indent the first line of a new paragraph to alert readers to such changes. Just as a period at the end of a sentence provides your readers with time to reflect upon your sentence, so a visual break of white space between paragraphs gives them proportionately more time to weigh the central meaning of a number of sentences.

Two types of paragraph are most commonly used in business and technical writing: *bridging* paragraphs and *developed* paragraphs.

A BRIDGING PARAGRAPHS

Bridging paragraphs provide transitions into and out of memos and letters, and are shorter than developed paragraphs. Often, they are only one sentence in length. You are probably most familiar with them as the first and last paragraphs in memos or letters.

The major use of a bridging paragraph is to introduce or to end a topic. You may also find them useful within a long letter to provide your readers with relief from a steady diet of long, developed paragraphs. Be careful not to string too many bridging paragraphs together, however, or your thought will strike the reader as sporadic and lightweight.

Examples of Bridging Paragraphs

> Thank you for your letter of July 9, asking for details of our tenant protection policy.
>
> —Opening paragraph in a response to an inquiry
>
> The basic skill in every profession and in most businesses is the ability to organize and express ideas in writing and in speaking.
>
> —Opening paragraph in a Royal Bank *Monthly Letter*
>
> If I can be of further assistance, please call me at (202) 414-6547.
>
> —Concluding paragraph in a Public Service letter

B *DEVELOPED PARAGRAPHS*

The developed paragraph develops meaning to a fuller extent than a bridging paragraph. When it is specific, coherent and unified, and uses power sentences, I term it the *power paragraph.*

Developed paragraphs usually consist of four or five sentences. First comes the *key sentence.* This establishes the core idea that the rest of the sentences in the paragraph develop. Next come three or four sentences, each of which adds an illustration or example to support the key sentence. Finally, the concluding sentence sums up the idea of the paragraph as a whole. If you keep this pattern in mind, you will write well-developed *power paragraphs.*

Analyze the above paragraph's structure for an illustration of a *power paragraph.*

*Examples of
Developed
Power
Paragraphs*

Key Sentence

Illustrations

Concluding
Sentence

Spending too little time organizing your writing can cost you money. Suppose you write a memo to 1,000 people, perhaps your employees or agents. You take one hour to block out the memo; your readers take an average of five minutes to read and understand it. On the other hand, suppose you were to spend two hours in composing the memo or letter, writing it so simply and briefly that your readers could absorb it in only four minutes. You would spend 60 extra minutes and your readers together would save 1,000 minutes. Taking a little longer to write clearly, you would have saved time, money and friendly feeling.

—Adapted from the Royal Bank *Monthly Letter*

In large organizations, such as government agencies, you may find your superiors disagree on how much detail you should include in reports. You may try to please your immediate boss by including as much detail as possible. She may be pleased, but the next one up the line says, "Too much detail burdens the reader. The assistant will never approve this." You spend a day removing the details, and the next boss up says, "Conclusions are unsupported by details." Such disagreements lie behind many cases of premature balding in young civil servants.

—Adapted from International Writing Institute's
Put It In Writing

Such perfectly structured paragraphs too rarely occur. Usually one or more of the elements are left out or shift position, marring the paragraph's *coherence.* Often irrelevant ideas intrude, destroying the paragraph's *unity.* However, if *you* master the skill of building coherent and unified paragraphs, you will soon be in high demand as a writer.

C *TRANSITIONAL MARKERS*

Just as signposts show the destination you will reach by taking certain roads while driving, so certain words and phrases tell your reader the direction your thought will take within the paragraph. Usually, these transitional markers occur at the beginning of a paragraph, and

List of Transitional Markers

Type Thought	Transitional Marker
Addition	again, also, finally, first, second, third, furthermore, in addition, last, likewise, next, too, then
Example	for example, for instance, in other words, specifically, such as, that is, to illustrate
Concession	after all, at the same time, even though, of course
Comparison	likewise, similarly, in turn, in a like manner, by the same token
Contrast	on the other hand, at the same time, but, on the contrary, nevertheless, still, yet, whereas
Cause/Effect	consequently, hence, in short, otherwise, since, so, then, therefore, thus, accordingly, as a result
Time	when, after, as soon as, at that time, before, now, later, meanwhile, presently, soon, while
Summary	in conclusion, in short, in essence, on the whole, in brief, to sum up

also at the beginning of sentences that take new directions within the paragraph. The list shows transitional markers grouped according to the type of thought they introduce. You will be selecting some of them for use in an exercise on attaining one of the key qualities in writing power paragraphs — coherence.

In an unusually long developed paragraph such as the following one, see how the transitional markers (printed in italics) act like signposts to help keep you on the right track, ensuring coherence.

Example: Transitional Markers Used to Establish Coherence

Memos and letters share certain qualities, but differ in important ways. The memo must speak clearly and concisely. *Likewise*, the letter will accomplish more if it makes its point quickly. *Both* types of communication strive for unity and coherence: *that is*, every sentence follows logically from the one before it. *In turn*, each sentence leads naturally into the one following. The two forms differ, *on the other hand*, in that the memo usually takes up half a page or less, is informal, and reaches internal correspondents, *whereas* the letter usually runs from one to two pages, is more formal, and communicates with those outside the organization. *Of course*, both forms perform important tasks in different ways. *In essence*, choose the one which suits your current audience.

The markers are of the following categories (in order): *comparison, example, comparison, contrast, contrast, contrast, concession, summary.*

COHERENCE AND UNITY

Transitional markers provide your chief tool in establishing *coherence*. Coherence means that each sentence connects easily and logically with the preceding one. Therefore, practice using a variety of transitional markers in your paragraphs to dovetail your sentences, guiding the reader easily along your paths of thought.

In addition to coherence, strive for *unity* in your paragraphs. Unity requires that all sentences illustrate or support the major thought expressed by the key sentence.

Example of a Unified Paragraph

In English, word order is crucial. Phrases can be arranged and rearranged like putty, turning nouns into verbs, verbs into nouns, nouns into adjectives. One can, as the *Encyclopaedia Brittanica* observes, plan a table or table a plan, book a place or place a book, lift a thumb or thumb a lift.

—*U.S. News & World Report*

Here the topic is word order, and every sentence and detail refers directly to that topic, providing the paragraph with the quality of unity.

When you write power paragraphs that contain the qualities of coherence and unity, you will make yourself easily understood, and your reader will respect and appreciate your style.

IV   *SECTION REVIEW*

You have studied how to achieve clarity through *power sentences*, coherence and unity through *power paragraphs*. If you now can recognize the nouns in a sentence, and know which is the subject and which is the object; if you can also distinguish between linking and action verbs; if you can replace generalized nouns and verbs with specific ones; if you can construct ideas in the form of developed paragraphs using clear transitional markers— then you are well on the way to becoming indispensable to your organization.

Writing is easy; all you do is sit staring at a blank sheet of paper until the drops of blood form on your forehead.
—Gene Fowler

While good writers know many additional grammatical techniques, the ability to write a clear sentence and a clear paragraph stand at the top of the list in terms of their importance to the writer and reader. In Section 2 you will learn how to write from the reader's point of view, and in Section 3 you will learn how to organize and research major writing projects, such as reports; however, both these skills depend on your ability to be clear in your individual sentences and paragraphs.

Therefore, the time you have invested in studying the principles explained here in Section 1 will pay you handsome dividends as you study the rest of this book and throughout your career.

V REFERENCE BOOKS: GRAMMAR

If you are interested in learning more about grammar and usage, here are some useful texts:

TECHNICAL WRITING TEXTS

Technical Writing, by Norman Levine. (New York: Harper and Row, 1978). A quick, reliable reference book. A lively, unpretentious style.

The Technician as Writer, by Ingrid Brunner. (Indianapolis: Bobbs-Merrill, 1983). A comprehensive handbook on reports.

GRAMMAR AND PUNCTUATION REFERENCE TEXTS

The Wordwatcher's Guide to Grammar and Good Writing, by Morton Freeman. (Cincinnati, Ohio: Writer's Digest Books, 1990).

The Canadian Writer's Handbook, by William E. Messenger and Jan de Bruyn. 2nd edition. (Scarborough, Ontario: Prentice-Hall, 1986). A thorough, reliable and clearly written reference tool.

Pinckert's Practical Grammar, by Robert C. Pinckert. (Cincinnati, Ohio: Writer's Digest Books, 1986).

The Bare Essentials, by Sarah Norton and Brian Green. (Toronto: Holt, Rinehart and Winston, 1980). A short and easily digested handbook.

BACKGROUND TEXT FOR TEACHERS

Teaching English Grammar, by Robert C. Pooley. (New York: Appleton-Century Crofts, 1957). Profoundly intelligent; exceptionally well-informed; a philosophy of grammar teaching that could serve as a model for all others.

MEASURING READABILITY

Robert Gunning's Fog Index is the easiest measurement of readability to use. Slightly adapted, it consists here of the following three steps:

1 Select a passage of 100 words or more, and divide the number of words by the number of sentences. This gives you the passage's average sentence length.
2 Count the number of polysyllables in the passage. Omit from this total proper nouns of more than three syllables (the names of people, products and organizations). Also omit three-syllable verbs which end with "ed" or "es," such as "projected" or "ensures."
3 Multiply the total of **1** and **2** by .4. This will give you the Fog Index of the passage.

The ideal Fog Index for business writing is between 10 and 14. Between 8 and 10 is acceptable. Over 14 is too heavy for most situations. Under 8 is too lightweight—except in the case of User Manual instructions, where a rating of 7-8 may be acceptable for the sake of maximum clarity.

VI *ANSWER KEY*

EXERCISE 1

*Recognizing
Subject- and
Object-Nouns*

Circle the subject-nouns, and underline the
object-nouns, in the following sentences.
Remember that the subject-noun *performs* the
action in the sentence, and that some of the
sentences are tricky.

1 (The memo) set forth seven purchase
options.

2 After several years of neglect, (he) organized
his budget.

3 My letter was cut in half by (the hard-nosed
editor.)

4 (Bill) conducted tests on the three-blade
propeller.

5 The analysis of results was presented by
(the field engineer.)

6 The financial statements for Stetson Inc.
were analyzed by the (accountant.)

7 (We) will sell our subsidiary companies in
two years.

8 (Mr. White's report) contained several errors.

9 (The company) fired all of its employees.

10 (George Marvin) received a pay increase
after he had worked 15 weeks.

11 A new personnel manager has been hired
by (the company.)

12 (The vice-president) asked me to handle the
Chadwick account.

13 The new (director of programming) started
his career as a radio announcer.

14 Before (we) can rent this car, we must make
  sure it is insured.

15 Several programs were run by (Joanne) at
  the seminar.

Note: Each of these nouns stands for the
person or thing doing the action in the
sentence—the origin of the energy that the
verb describes.

EXERCISE 2

Circle the linking verbs. Rewrite the sentences,
replacing the linking verbs with action verbs.

*Changing
Linking Verbs
to Action
Verbs*

1 The second memo (is) sixteen pages longer
  than the first one.
  *The second memo contains sixteen pages
  more than the first one.*

2 The president and the executive committee
  (are) in agreement.
  *The president agrees with the executive
  committee* or
  *The president and executive committee
  agree.*

3 The lieutenant (will be) an effective leader of
  the men.
  The lieutenant will lead the men effectively.

4 Jim (was) pleased with the children's
  development.
  The children's development pleased Jim.

5 This layout (will be) satisfactory to the staff.
  This layout will satisfy (or, please) *the staff.*

6 With a word processor, you (are) free to shift
  text around.
  *A word processor allows you to shift text
  around.*

7 The chief executive officer(is)quick to adopt new methods.

The chief executive officer adopts new methods quickly.

8 Janice(is)an efficient computer programmer.

Janice programs computers efficiently.

9 Alex(is)responsible for investigating all accidents that occur on company premises.

Alex investigates all accidents that occur on company premises.

10 A comprehensive management training program(is)useful for all employees.

All employees will benefit from a comprehensive management training program.

11 The assessment team(was)in a meeting at the Pacific Hotel.

The assessment team met at the Pacific Hotel.

12 Each employee(is)ready for work by 9 a.m.

Each employee begins work by 9 a.m.

13 Alice(was)well qualified for the position of credit manager.

The position of credit manager suited Alice's qualifications.

14 The air(is)cold and wet.

The air feels cold and wet.

15 The courier(was)late bringing the new contracts.

The courier brought the new contracts late.

EXERCISE 3

***Rewriting in
the Active
Voice***

Using the three-step procedure outlined in the
table entitled "How to Locate the Subject-
Noun," circle the grammatical subject in each
of these sentences; then rewrite each
sentence, if necessary, in the active voice
pattern.

1 The public information officer was misled
by (the letter.)

*The letter misled the public information
officer.*

2 The field staff were delighted by (the)
(supervisor's appointment.)

*The supervisor's appointment delighted the
field staff.*

3 (Bill) engineered the satellite tracking
antenna.

[*This sentence is already in the active
voice.*]

4 "Why bother?" drawled (Sleepy.)

Sleepy drawled, "Why bother?"

5 A copy of the report is sent by (the client.)

The client sent a copy of the report.

6 Disciplinary action is taken by (the)
(supervisor) after thoroughly investigating
the incident.

*The supervisor takes disciplinary action
after thoroughly investigating the incident.*

7 Administrative staff are authorized by (the)
(company) to ensure that employees
conform to the company's dress code.

*The company authorizes administrative
staff to ensure that employees conform to
the company's dress code.*

8 Two probationary reviews are written by (the manager) for each employee.

The manager writes two probationary reviews for each employee.

9 Andrea was dismayed by (Mr. Aiken's poor) (reaction to her presentation.)

Mr. Aiken's poor reaction to her presentation dismayed Andrea.

10 You will be presented with a free sample from (our company.)

Our company will present you with a free sample.

11 New employees will be advised by (the) (department head) regarding the location of their lockers.

The department head will advise new employees regarding the location of their lockers.

12 Six employees were honored with (a long) (service recognition ceremony.)

A long service recognition ceremony honored six employees.

13 A trip to Japan was received by (Joe) (Morgan) for his outstanding sales record last year.

Joe Morgan received a trip to Japan for his outstanding sales record last year.

14 All overtime hours must be confirmed by (the employee's department head.)

The employee's department head must confirm all overtime hours.

EXERCISE 4

Changing the Passive to the Active Voice

Circle the grammatical subject-nouns of the following sentence, where present. Underline the objects. Double-underline the verbs. Provide a subject-noun if needed, and rewrite all the sentences in subject—verb—object order, using action verbs.

1 Labor peace has been sought.

No subject present (divine passive).
[The contractor] sought labor peace.

2 A way will be found to master this material.

No subject present.
[They]'ll find a way to master this material.

3 Susan is considered a successful negotiator.

No subject present.
[We] consider Susan a successful negotiator.

4 One was struck by (the clock.)

Subject: clock.
The clock struck one.

5 The moon was jumped over by (the cow.)

Subject: the cow.
The cow jumped over the moon.

6 (Sam) weighed the alternatives and made a decision.

Subject: Sam. No change needed.

7 Grievances are handled in accordance with the step approach method.

No subject present.
[The company] handles grievances in accordance with the step approach method.

8 Every effort will be made to handle problems as they arise.

No subject present.
[The manager] will make every effort to handle problems as they arise.

9 The safety rules are designed to ensure employees avoid accidents.

No subject present.
[The company] designs safety rules to ensure employees avoid accidents.

10 Employees are advised by (management) not to bring excessive amounts of money or valuables to the workplace.

Management advises employees not to bring excessive amounts of money or valuables to the workplace.

11 Vacation times are allocated in accordance with each employee's years of service to the company.

No subject present.
[The personnel department] allocates vacation times in accordance with each employee's years of service to the company.

12 There is nothing to be done about our high absentee rate.

No subject present.
[We] can do nothing about our high absentee rate.

13 You were asked to submit the report no later than 3 p.m. on Tuesday, December 22.

No subject present.
[We] asked you to submit the report no later than 3 p.m. on Tuesday, December 22.

14 Sick leave is payable only when a regular full- or part-time employee is absent from work as a result of an illness or non-work related injury.

No subject present.
[The company] pays sick leave only when a regular full- or part-time employee is absent from work as a result of an illness or non-work related injury.

15 Requests for credit information regarding company employees are received in writing.

No subject present.
[We] must receive written requests for credit information regarding company employees.

EXERCISE 5

Writing the Power Sentence

Turn this passive voice sentence into a power sentence:
The course was talked about by the people concerned.

S—V—O

1 *The people concerned talked about the seminar.*

Action Verb

2 *The people concerned* praised *the seminar.*

Specifics

3 *The* secretaries *praised the* Written Power *seminar.*

EXERCISE 6

Punctuation

Apply the rules of punctuation to correct the following sentences.

1 As soon as I arrived, I corrected the punctuation in my letter.

2 The personnel manager will advertise the position; the vice-president will conduct the interviews.

3 Meet us on the fifth floor—not the fourth floor—in three hours.

4 The client thanked Ms. Martin [Marten] for her excellent report.

5 Secondly, I would like to discuss how my proposal will increase profits.

2 *UNDERSTANDING YOUR READER*

OBJECTIVES:

- Generate Good Will in Memos and Letters

- Adopt the You Attitude

- Prefer the Positive Approach

- Write with a Human Touch

- Structure Letters Correctly

- Handle Letter Layout Correctly

- Use Non-Sexist Language

INTRODUCTION

In the first section you learned how to write *clearly*. This section shows how to write *effectively*. You can see the difference by asking yourself what you think of someone who continually orders you about. They may be perfectly clear in saying, "Send me all vacation leave entitlements in your region," or "Get back to me by Tuesday." But what about their tone? Most people produce better work when they are asked rather than told to do something. The effective communicator, therefore, displays sensitivity to the other person's way of looking at things. This section will show you how to write effectively by phrasing your messages from the reader's point of view.

Two main qualities of writing are required to make letters effective:

1 A *Tone* of good will
2 An effective *Structure.*

Writers create a tone of good will by using these three techniques:

1 The You Attitude
2 The Positive Approach
3 The Human Touch.

Similarly, writers structure letters effectively by careful attention to these two considerations:

1 Psychological layout
2 Physical layout.

After working through this section, you will know how to guarantee that both the tone and structure of your letters will have a favorable impact on your readers.

I *A TONE OF GOOD WILL*

Strive to write memos and letters that either *generate or retain good will* in your reader. Alternatives to this approach are not attractive. They consist of generating one of the following two attitudes in the reader:

1 ill will
2 bare tolerance.

Caesar is above grammar.
—Frederick the Great

"But why should I bother? I'm in control here." True, but although your subordinates may not be in a position to resist decisions you make in your official capacity, you run an unnecessary risk when you write uncaringly, abruptly, or officiously. On the other hand, if you promote good will in all communications, you will benefit later—perhaps in unexpected ways.

Generating good will may seem irrelevant when you are not asking your reader to give you anything immediate or specific in return, such as a refund, a job, or a reference. For example, many memos simply provide a list of information, give instructions, or order supplies. Do you have anything to gain personally by generating good will at all times?

If you think about it a little more deeply than people usually do, you will see that in fact you *are* asking your reader for something important in situations like this—to accept your information or instructions in a spirit of good will and perhaps to act on them. A reader who receives an abrupt, insensitive memo will be reluctant to cooperate.

Perhaps you will see the results of this friction at some point during your career. A reader may grudgingly carry out your order, request further clarification endlessly, "work to rule," gossip destructively, or complain to superiors or to outside agencies. Even though you may ask nothing specific of your readers, you do depend to some extent on their willingness to give your message an open-minded hearing. A spirit of good will is the *prerequisite* for successful tone in communication.

Now that we've mentioned the advantages of creating a general climate of good will in your letters, we can turn to the three attributes which, when combined, create a tone of good will. Just as learning to write the power sentence in Section 1 required you to recognize three key attributes (the active voice, action verbs and specific words), so learning how to create an effective tone requires you to attain detailed mastery of three key techniques: the You Attitude, the Positive Approach and the Human Touch.

To make it easier for you to acquire these key techniques, we'll describe each of them in their turn, and provide examples. Why not pull out a file of your own letters to see if you already employ good tone, as you study each of its aspects? At the end of this discussion of tone, we'll move on to the study of effective structure. Your file of letters will come in handy there, too.

A *THE YOU ATTITUDE*

To write your letters and memos from your reader's point of view, ensure that your sentences frequently begin with your *reader's name*, or the word "*you*." Cut down on the number of sentences that begin with the words "I," or "We" or the name of your organization. For example, instead of saying, "*I* agree with you," write "*You* are correct."

What is the difference? In English, the subject-noun near the beginning of a sentence occupies the place of greatest impact. By putting words which refer to your reader in this privileged position, and also adopting a polite and considerate tone, you show respect. In a sense, you are putting the reader's name in bright lights, instead of your own.

CALCULATING YOUR "YOU ATTITUDE"

Here is a way to calculate the You Attitude in your writing. Take out a letter or memo you have written recently; then perform the following calculations:

---

1 Total the number of sentences that begin with the word "we," the word "I," or with the name of your organization.

2 Total the number of sentences that begin with the word "you," or your reader's name, or the name of your reader's organization.

Do your "you" sentences outnumber "we" sentences by at least three to one? If so, your letters convey a strong "you" attitude.

Of course, the "you" statements must be *positive* ones in order to qualify. Don't say things like this: "If you had followed our instructions correctly, you wouldn't be in *trouble* now." (Not what we're aiming for!)

This calculation will help you to express ideas from your reader's point of view—the chief virtue of the You Attitude. For example, instead of writing, "*Our* annual report will undoubtedly supply you with the statistics you asked for," write, "*You* will find the statistics you asked for in our annual report." Readers feel that you have seen things from their perspective when you use this method—and you have!

The more you practice the You Attitude, the better you will become at seeing situations from the point of view of various readers. You will achieve your goal of communicating effectively if you adopt this approach.

Let's analyze a sentence from a typical letter:

Dear Customer:

It was only after a great deal of thought and effort that *we* were able to come up with this inexpensive overdraft protection plan that *we* think will benefit *our* new customers, such as yourself.

Can you see how the use of "we" conveys a self-concerned attitude on the part of the writer ("We, we, our")? A simple change of viewpoint leads to this:

Dear Mr. Inkster:

You will find the enclosed overdraft protection plan very economical, offering *you* maximum security.

This "you" version uses the reader's name (where possible) and presents benefits from the *reader's* point of view. Which version would you rather receive?

EXERCISE 7   Underline the words in this letter which refer to the writer. Then rewrite the letter with the You Attitude, and check your version against the answer key, page 95.

Dear Mr. Winfield:

We are in receipt of your letter requesting permission to franchise our product in Utah. We always appreciate receiving a letter from agents who wish to handle our soap. We have received more submissions than we can easily handle.

In any case, I am afraid that it is against our policy to sell distributor rights to more than one franchisee in cities of fewer than 7,000, and as Mr. Hicraft is already open for business in Crow Creek, I regret we cannot authorize another agency.

If we decide to change our marketing policy we will contact you. We will keep your name on file for six months.

Sincerely,
Derek Jones

The You Attitude

The following paragraph uses the word "you." Does it express the You Attitude?:

Dear Cardholder:

We are writing to notify you that your account is overdue. You owe us $2,454.67. Our records show that although you have been a cardholder for less than one year, your payments have frequently been received late. This is unacceptable to us.

If you said "NO!," you're correct. As you can see, negative thinking and the "we attitude" predominate, subverting the effect of using the words "you" and "your." Such unenlightened business writing will not assist sales of the company's services in today's competitive marketplace. It might have been better written in this way:

Dear Mr. Thompson,

Please note that your outstanding balance of $2,454.67 on your account with us was not paid last month. This has happened three times over the last year. Please make your payments on time in the future, so that we will be able to keep your account active.

Here is another example. What do you think?:

THANK YOU for alerting us to your circulation problem. We are checking our records and will make the appropriate adjustment to your subscription immediately.

It often takes from four to six weeks for changes to be integrated into our master subscriber file, but please be assured that your problem has been taken care of—ignore any incorrect invoices or renewal notices in the interim.

Your correction will be effective with Issue No. 66. Thank you for your patience.

Sincerely,
Circulation Department

YES, this letter represents an excellent use of the You Attitude. It builds reader confidence in the company's willingness and ability to serve its clients well. Writing with the You Attitude in this way is well worth the effort, and will come with a little patience.

B   *THE POSITIVE APPROACH*

Have you noticed that open-minded people and organizations employ the Positive Approach, as well as the You Attitude? They think, talk and act as though things were possible. They create interesting directions out of chaos, inspired solutions out of difficulty. They radiate lightness, energy and humor—as they fulfill their potential.

Close-minded people and organizations adopt a negative approach. They talk as though things were difficult—or impossible. They doubt, dwell on difficulties, and use rules to guide every action. They refuse to consider problems as possible of solution, and they radiate arrogance, sarcasm and fear alternately.

Which attitude does your writing style convey to your readers? Which attitude puts your reader into the most receptive mood?

Since you are studying this material in the attempt to improve your ability as a communicator, you are engaged in a positive effort. Therefore, it makes sense that you continue to demonstrate this positive effort in your correspondence by making your tone as positive as possible.

However, the positive attitude is often unnatural. Just as babies have to learn to fight gravity to stand upright, so we have to fight negativity to speak positively. Positive attitudes arise from education, not from chance. You can convince yourself of this by recalling typical remarks around the office. What is the ratio of positive to negative comments? In most areas of life, negative thinking dominates. Think of the typical content of TV news programs and daily newspapers!

On the other hand, educated people prize the positive attitude, like gold, for its rarity, beauty, durability. One popular regional manager, when asked for the theory which accounted for his outstanding success with people, offered this simple phrase: "*A pat on the back is eighteen inches higher than a kick in the pants.*" This vivid advice to act positively illustrates the connection between success and positive thinking.

In order to cultivate this kind of positive attitude, learn to replace negative—or even neutral—words with positive ones. For example, instead of saying, "Please do not *hesitate* to call me," you could say, "Please feel *free* to call me," or, "Please call me." Similarly, instead of saying, "We *regret* that we cannot continue to provide credit until you *send* us your overdue payment," you could say, "We will be *glad* to provide credit as soon as we *receive* the payment due." Of course, you must use your discretion to avoid effusiveness.

WHY PREFER POSITIVE WORDS?

Psychologists have found that people remember negative thoughts more vividly than positive ones, perhaps because negative thoughts are stored in an ancient, unsophisticated part of the brain (the limbic system). Studies of memory show that major errors or failures (negative thoughts) are five times more easily recalled over a period of three years than pleasant memories or successes (positive thoughts). This may explain why it is five times harder to build a good reputation than to lose it!

Negative Words to Avoid

argue, argument	fail (failures)
bad	fault
bill (verb)	late
claim (verb)	reject
complain	sorry
debt	strictly
defect	submit
delay	terrible
difficult (difficulties)	wasted
doubt	wrong
embarrassed	hesitate
error	worthless
careless	problem

Note: The words "no" and "not" are not classified as negative words. They are used together with positive words to convey unwelcome messages positively.

EXERCISE 8   Find and underline all negative words in the
                      following memo.

                      Some couriers have carelessly sent all their
                      undelivered parcels on to the Halifax depot for
                      storage. This has created several problems.

                      Therefore, supervisors should eradicate any
                      worthless parcels before forwarding them. The
                      Halifax depot suffers from the general space
                      problems too. We are not a garbage dump.

                      Do not hesitate to submit further difficulties to this
                      office for inclusion in our list of problem areas within
Identifying   the organization.
Negative
Words   Check your answers with the answer key, page
                      96.

___

     Positive words include "glad," "pleased,"
"happy," "improvements," "service,"
"contribution." Use positive words to express
unwelcome ideas: "Our *service* to you did *not
meet the high standards* we expect of our
staff." Here the use of "not" allows us to use
the positive words "meet the high standards."
Expressed negatively, we might have written,
"Our service *failed* to meet *minimal* standards
for treatment of customers." Readers react
more favorably to the positive wording.

___

DETERMINING YOUR NEGATIVE—
POSITIVE RATIO

Tone
Evaluation   ┌──────────────────────────────────────┐
Procedure   │ 1 Multiply the negative words in a letter │
                      │   you have written by five;   │
                      │ 2 Multiply the number of positive words in │
                      │   the same letter by one.   │
                      └──────────────────────────────────────┘

These totals provide your Negative/Positive word ratio.

What should my ratio be?

Here is a guide with which to interpret the tone of your writing:

Tone Interpretation Guide

	Negative Total	Positive Total
Excellent	0	6+
Good	5	5
Unsatisfactory	10-15	5
Poor	15+	5

Good writers often use no negative words. The higher the number of negative words in your letter now, the more challenging this recommendation may seem, but persevere, and your readers will appreciate the difference. (However, do not call rate increases "new rates" unless you provide specifics for comparison. Readers resent manipulation.)

C *THE HUMAN TOUCH*

Many business letters sound indifferent, superior, or wooden. The Human Touch refers to the quality of writing that makes your letters sound as though they were written from one living, breathing, caring individual to another. Just as you have a distinct tone of voice on the telephone or in person, so you have your own tone in writing. If you get stuck on tone when trying to phrase a letter, stop and rest for a bit. Call up to your mind's eye the image of your best friend, and pretend you're talking to him or her directly, person to person. Remember the words you would use in that happy situation, and write them down. You can't be pompous or wooden when talking to good friends. They won't stand for it! This technique will ensure that your letters display the Human Touch.

You have your own Human Touch. I can't anticipate what it will feel like. However, here are two very different examples of the Human Touch, to show you how very differently two people can write when they let their writing style express their personalities.

A SOPHISTICATED EXAMPLE

The first example comes from a highly respected business writer of the more conservative type, writing to a conservative banking audience. Here he warns against some poor habits of writing. His style is recognizable and distinct, and expresses his gracefully old-fashioned personality:

> The writer will, in his re-reading, harden his heart to his felicitous phrases and his smoothly flowing paragraphs. He will be alert to censure spiritless sentences, condemn what is rugged and misshapen, draw a line through what is incorrect factually, lop off redundant words and phrases while preserving the virtues of repetition, remove distracting ornament, rearrange what is expressed ambiguously, and throw light upon the parts that are difficult to understand. One needs the sort of hard-hearted determination voiced by Ovid when he said, "When I re-read I blush, for even I perceive enough that ought to be erased, though it was I who wrote the stuff."
> —The Royal Bank *Monthly Letter*

Notice that the author writes lengthy sentences, employs a fairly sophisticated level of diction ("felicitous"), and quotes the classical Roman writer Ovid. Therefore, he thinks of his audience as educated and sophisticated. Nevertheless, he speaks sensibly, uses strong Action verbs, and makes good points. This passage expresses one extreme of acceptable business writing, where your audience appreciates intricacy of phrasing and reference.

A COLLOQUIAL EXAMPLE

Here is a much more colloquial passage from a second writer. Joe Girard is a self-made salesman with little formal education. His sentences are crisp, purposely ungrammatical at times ("I made me [myself] a salesman"), but they unabashedly express his own enthusiasm and knowledge of selling:

> Somebody once told me that I was a born salesman. Let me tell you that's not true. Some salesmen, maybe even most salesmen, may be born to it. But I was not born a salesman. I made me a salesman, all by myself. And if I could do it, starting from where I did, anybody can. Stay with this story and you'll see what I mean.
> —Joe Girard, *How to Sell Anything to Anybody*

Mr. Girard thinks of his audience as relatively uneducated, but full of energy, intention and purpose. He writes to put them at their ease, and to encourage them, by making them see that they do not require perfect grammar to become successful salespeople.

I don't recommend that you adopt a style as formal as the first, or as informal as the second. However, whatever their drawbacks, both writers have found a gracious or a lively tone that expresses their individuality.

In seeking to develop your own style, try to write with a tone similar to that which you use on the telephone, though more carefully worded and organized. This care is necessary because written messages may undergo a close and lasting scrutiny.

SHOULD YOU USE YOUR READER'S NAME?

Yes, attempt to use your reader's name in the body of your letter at least once—even when composing form letters. Dale Carnegie often said that the sound of a person's name has a sweet ring to it in their own ears. Although sales letters sometimes repeat the reader's name too many times, perhaps, most people like to see their own name in print. Just be sure to spell it correctly! In particular, check to see that if you have presented their name in the inside address of your letter, you have also used it in the salutation.

WRITING FOR THE BOSS

One of the most difficult tasks you may ever face is to be asked to write a letter for someone else, such as your manager. This is a special talent, like that of a ventriloquist. How do you imitate their Human Touch? Some people can do it easily; others cannot. Remember, if you get discouraged trying to write in this way, that letters you write for another person cannot be as comfortably written as those you write for yourself. So simply do your best, and improve by examining and imitating the tone of your manager's corrections.

One new alternative that has received growing acceptance is to write the letter in your own voice, and then type your manager's name underneath the complimentary close in the normal way. However, instead of your manager signing it, *you* do, underneath the word "by." This approach retains the manager's responsibility for content, while leaving the writer responsible for style. Use of this system demonstrates the manager's confidence in you as a writer.

Example of a Letter Written on behalf of a Manager

March 4, 1992

Ms. S. Buckingham
1615 Travis Drive
Portland, Maine
01345

Dear Sue,

Here is the letter you requested from our Director of Financial Services regarding your contract extension.

To clarify our agreement, we confirm our order of two seminars on business writing a week for twelve weeks, on the dates we selected last Tuesday.

I hope this clarifies our understanding. If you require any additional information over the next three weeks, please contact Sandra Ludwig at 787-1453. She will be handling these affairs while I'm away on medical leave.

Best wishes for a successful completion of our training strategy.

Yours truly,

Bill Gibson
Manager, Employee Planning

by:

W.O. Simpson
Staff Development Officer
Management Development

Here the manager has accepted responsibility for the content of the letter, but the author, W.O. Simpson, has signed it to accept responsibility for the style.

EXERCISE 9

Write a letter instructing a subordinate how to handle a procedure which you know well. Read the letter aloud; then revise it to bring the written words closer to your style of conversation over the telephone. In particular,

**Developing
Your Human
Touch**

remove all trace of superiority, authoritarianism
and woolliness. Ensure that you use the other
person's name at least once. Then give your
letter to a colleague, and ask if it *sounds* like
you. *Your* style will surface if you do this
conscientiously three or four times.

D SUMMARY OF TONE

You have studied how to generate good will
through the use of the You Attitude, the
Positive Approach, and the Human Touch.
These qualities will establish a communication
context favorable to your message.
Congratulations on your hard work! To this
point, you know how to write clearly and
effectively. There is one remaining challenge:
Effective Structure. You may want to run
around the block before settling down to learn
how to say "Yes" and "No" in the appropriate
sequence.

II *LETTER STRUCTURE*

Good writers take two main components into consideration when structuring letters:

1 Psychological layout
2 Physical layout.

Each of these components contributes to the impact of your letters.

A *PSYCHOLOGICAL LAYOUT*

The structure of a letter will vary depending on the psychological thrust of the communication —whether you're asking the reader to accept good or bad news. Psychologists have found that you should sequence messages differently depending on whether they contain information that will strike the reader as welcome ("good" news) or unwelcome ("bad" news). For this learning session, we will term "good" news letters "YES" letters, and "bad" news letters "NO" letters.

THE YES LETTER

The YES letter either gives good news *or* provides information that moves business matters forward. NOTE: Consider all informational memos and letters as YES letters for the purpose of structuring.

The most effective order for the YES letter is as follows:

YES

> 1 Say YES
> 2 Supply necessary details
> 3 Close in a friendly way

Let's take a look at the reasoning behind this, realizing that it is normal human behavior to say "yes" last—not first. Many letter writers feel that if they say "yes" first the reader will not finish reading the letter they have labored over. However, it is not in your best interest to make your reader anxious before receiving welcome news. You will serve your reader's interests best by providing a positive response as soon as possible—usually in the first paragraph. As with the You Attitude, this necessitates seeing things from the reader's viewpoint.

Example of the YES Letter

February 28, 1992

Mr. G. L. Hammersham
4342 Maryland Way
New York, New York
04345

Dear Mr. Hammersham,

Yes

Thank you for your letter of February 14, requesting "a replacement steering wheel for a 1986 Buick Century." Our factory shipped your wheel to you today.

Details

Your letter did not specify whether you wanted the tan or the ivory edging. I have shipped the tan selection, which was the color of the original part. If you require ivory, please return the tan edging for replacement.

Positive close

You should receive your part within five working days. Please let me know if I can be of further help. Our toll-free line is 1-800-555-6789, and you can order by phone seven days a week.

Sincerely,

Jim Foster
Shipping Facilitator

EXERCISE 10

Writing the
YES Letter

Write a letter containing good news, following the structure for the YES letter. Bracket in pen the three stages of your letter, and write the name of each stage (Yes, details, close) in the margin.

THE NO LETTER

The NO letter may be defined as any letter which either imparts unwelcome news, or which slows business activity. Complaint letters, rejection letters, and "Sorry, we're out of it" letters fall into this category.

Because people do not like to write these letters, those who write them skillfully are extremely valuable to an organization. To succeed, remember that you can often **assist** people by saying "No." One example of this is in the case of a request for credit where evidence exists that the applicant could not handle it properly. A second example is needing to refuse a job application from someone not suited to the job.

Remember that in this kind of NO letter the three elements of good tone—the You Attitude, the Positive Approach, and the Human Touch —are even more useful than in the YES letter. This is worth repeating: Keep NO letters positive in tone, speak with the You Attitude, and maintain your Human Touch. If you can do all this, even your NO letter will leave a good impression.

The NO   The most effective sequence for the NO letter
Structure   is as follows:

---

1 Say thank you for the request
2 State the context governing the decision,
   so *the reader* is prepared for the
   conclusion

NO   3 Say NO graciously (or clearly infer it)
4 Provide a positive alternative where
   possible
5 Close positively

As you can see, this sequence avoids saying
NO first. Inexperienced writers say NO first—
and then provide explanation or context, when
the reader may feel too emotionally downcast
to listen to reasonable explanations. Attempt to
have readers reach the conclusion before you
state it, so that by the time you say NO, they
are thinking, "Well, I already knew that." This
gives readers time to protect their ego; this
delay is particularly important in cases where
readers have invested a great deal in a positive
response from your organization.

How to Say   To establish your method of saying NO in
NO   letters, carefully weigh these considerations.
Firstly, always make it clear that you are
rejecting an idea or a proposal or a single
element of a person's character, and *not* the
person themselves. For example, instead of
saying, "There were several applicants who
were more suitable than you," say, "There
were several applicants whose *credentials* in
marketing exceeded yours." Here you are
talking about only one aspect of a person:
credentials in marketing. In short, always
refuse *things* rather than *people* in NO letters.
   Secondly, always speak as though the
position applied for—rather than you as a

person—requires certain characteristics that the unsuccessful applicant lacks. Say, "This position requires an expert in financial planning," rather than "*We* require an expert in financial planning" or "*I* require an expert in financial planning." In this way you make it clear that you have not rejected the person due to any personal disapproval.

Thirdly, give only the single main reason for rejection, and—where possible—have it apply to the area in which the person could most usefully improve. For example, in a case where an otherwise qualified and suitable applicant has had a number of poor references, say, "*One* of the main things this position requires is an excellent job history," rather than, "Job history, academic credentials, and length of service are the *three* main things we look for in applicants." This "one-shot" technique is called the "rifle approach," as opposed to the shotgun approach, where you list a multitude of deficiencies.

Where negative news is involved, the reader will scan your list outlining his or her shortcomings. If they find one item on this list is not completely correct, your entire letter will be discontinued as prejudiced. This can lead to costly appeals of your decisions when awarding jobs or contracts, for example. On the other hand, if you mention only one key element your letter will gain acceptance more quickly—and may result in personal improvement that will benefit everyone.

Lastly, keep the wording positive. Say, "Mr. Elton, your application was one of many we received from *extremely qualified people*," rather than "Mr. Elton, your application was one of hundreds we received." Say, "The *successful* applicant's credentials were *extremely impressive*," rather than, "Your credentials were *comparatively poor*." Positive wording counts greatly in this kind of letter.

**Example of
the NO Letter**

January 30, 1992

Ms. Esmeralda Somerset
1704 Mainstream Avenue
Kentucky, Illinois
64950

Dear Ms. Somerset,

Buffer

    Thank you for your application for a position as an agency representative with our firm.

Context details

    As you may know, Ms. Somerset, this position requires a great deal of experience in dealing with people who can be extremely aggressive and dismissive. Consequently, applications from those who have handled similar positions in the past have a distinct advantage.

No

    In the case of this opening, there was an excellent, experienced candidate who has been selected.

Positive
alternative

    However, your application impressed the selection panel strongly. They have asked me to suggest that you submit another application after a further year's experience.

Positive close

    Esmeralda, thank you for your excellent application. I wish you good luck with your career development, and hope to hear from you in one year.

Yours sincerely,

T.L. Champion
Vice President, Marketing

EXERCISE 11

Write a NO letter that involves something important to the reader. Use the correct structure, keep the proper tone, and include all the elements mentioned above. Identify each of the five stages in the letter by using brackets in the margin. Revise to ensure that the wording is neither negative *nor neutral*, but as sincere and positive—though never saccharine—as you can make it.

**Writing the
NO letter**

B *PHYSICAL LAYOUT*

As well as the psychological effect of tone and structure, it is important to be able to format letters correctly on the page and to use salutations and complimentary closes correctly. As with spelling, educated readers often judge writers on the basis of their knowledge of forms and layout.

LETTER FORMAT

There are a number of formats for business letters. Each of them is designed to present the message clearly and attractively. Here are two major ones: the *full block* style with no paragraph indentations and the *modified block* style with paragraph indentions.

A traditional argument in favor of eliminating indentions (full block) is that it saves typing time, and therefore costs less. However, the effect on the reader is not as pleasing as the modified block: the eye likes the breaks from full lines of print provided by paragraph indentations. Choose the format appropriate for your purposes and audience.

The following letter uses Full Block format to convey a NO message. [*NOTE:* The tone of this letter is extremely poor.]

Full Block Layout

Date	February 2, 1992
3 or more blank lines	
Inside address	Clean Construction, Inc. 1819 Turnstile Place Rivers, N. Carolina 24335
Att'n line	Att'n: T. Whitehead

Subject line

Account Number:	333-443433-35449
Previous Balance:	$1,344.65
Credits:	.00
Balance Due:	$1,344.65

Salutation

Dear Cardmember:

Body

We are writing to notify you that your account is overdue. You owe us $1,344.65. Our records show that although you have been a Cardmember for less than one year, your payments have frequently been received late. This is unacceptable to us.

The United Payment Card is a charge card, not a credit card. Our terms call for payment in full upon receipt of each monthly statement. This requirement was clearly indicated to you in the Cardmember Agreement that you received with the Card.

The United Payment Card is not for everyone. Charges are approved based on your past spending and payment record. We value you as a Cardmember but, if your late payments continue, we will consider suspending your charge privileges. Please mail your check today for the full balance due. If it is in the mail, thank you.

Complimentary close
CORP. NAME

Sincerely,
UNITED PAYMENT CARDS LIMITED

Signature

C. M. C. Reid

Typed name
Business title of writer

M. Reid
Card Account Services

Ref. initials

MR:aak

The second example uses the Modified Block format for a YES letter. Note the excellent tone.

Semi-block Layout

Date

Inside address

Salutation

Body

Complimentary close

Signature

Typed name
Business title of writer

February 25, 1992

Rosalind McCloud
1818 Greenhill Avenue
South Hills
Ontario, N7B 8X5

Dear Rosalind:

We received your letter letting us know you want to stop being in the Financial Family, and have adjusted our records accordingly. Enclosed are tax receipts for your 1990 and 1991 contributions.

As the person on staff who is responsible for our communications, I was particularly interested in your comments about the "depersonalization" you have noticed. My commitment is that we always speak person to person, and I would appreciate any specific comments you could make that would point to where we are not doing so.

Rosalind, your stand for the end of hunger is clear in your letter and in your commitment to Families for Children. Your contributions have also made the work of The Hunger Project possible, and I treasure our partnership in calling forth the end of hunger in our world, forever.

Yours truly,

John Boyle

John Boyle
Director of Communications

SALUTATIONS AND COMPLIMENTARY CLOSES

Within the format you choose, whether Full Block, Modified Block, or an in-house style, you have a number of salutations and complimentary closes to choose from. They can be grouped into four levels of descending formality, as follows:

Common Salutations & Complimentary Closes

Very Formal	
Sir:	Very respectfully yours,
Madam:	Yours respectfully,
	Respectfully,

Formal	
Dear Ms. Butterfield:	Very truly yours,
Dear Sir/Madam:	Yours truly,
[Note: "Madam" is	Yours respectfully,
outdated, but no alternative	
has yet arisen.]	

Normal	
Dear Peter Johnson,	Sincerely yours,
Dear Ms. Spokander,	Yours sincerely,
Dear Mr. Hudson,	Sincerely,
Dear L.Y. Harrison,	Yours truly,
[Used when the person's sex	
is not known]	

Personal or Friendly Business	
Dear Mary,	Most sincerely,
Dear Paul,	Yours cordially,
Dear Tom,	Cordially,
Dear Client,	Regards,
Dear Customer,	Best regards,
Dear Reader,	Yours,
Dear Friend,	

C   *NON-SEXIST LANGUAGE*

Good writers take care not to irritate their readers. This means using non-sexist language. Until this usage becomes more common it may seem a bit awkward, much as the use of "Ms." seemed odd to some writers when it replaced "Mrs." and "Miss" in the '70s. However, your time will be well invested learning this new style—artificial though it may seem at first.

1st Case:

Change the third person singular pronoun "he" to the third person pronoun plural. Instead of "Ask the client to send in *his* order," say "Ask clients to send in *their* orders." Caution: Avoid a lack of agreement such as this: "Every student must send in *their* application." Instead, write "*Students* must send in their applications."

2nd Case:

Change the third person singular to the second person singular "you." Instead of "The supervisor is responsible for posting *his* time schedule monthly," say "*You* are responsible for posting *your* time schedule monthly."

3rd Case:

Change "his" to "his or her." Instead of "Each writer has *his* own style," say "Each writer has *his* or *her* own style."

4th Case:

When writing job descriptions, replace "he" and "his" with a series of phrases which do not require subjects. Traditionally, a job description might read like this: "The administrator will be responsible for setting *his* department's policy, coordinating public statements, administering *his* budget effectively, and codifying *his* hiring procedures." Simply rewrite this in a series of phrases:

"The administrator will be responsible for the following:
1. Setting department policy
2. Coordinating public statements
3. Administering the budget effectively
4. Codifying hiring procedures."

5th Case:
Change job titles where appropriate.
"Salesman" becomes "Sales representative,"
"Mailman" = "Mail carrier," "Stewardess" =
"Flight attendant," "Chairman" =
"Chairperson."

Like every major change in language, these new usages may seem awkard for a few years; however, the principle of writing in a non-sexist way has been gaining broad public acceptance more quickly than many people once believed possible. By adopting this new style graciously, you can demonstrate your respect for all your readers.

D SUMMARY

You have seen how certain techniques of tone and structure can help you become a better letter writer. As with any skill, however, the spirit with which you undertake your task counts infinitely more than the precise adherence to rules. Always fine-tune the general recommendations about tone, in order to match your personality and suit your reader's needs.

*All things
excellent are
as difficult as
they are rare.*
—Spinoza

I am confident that you will find that the You Attitude, the Positive Approach, and the Human Touch will improve the quality of your communication with all your readers, as it has for many others. When you add the proper psychological and physical layout, your messages will be extremely effective. Now it's up to you to put this knowledge to work!

III ANSWER KEY

EXERCISE 7   Underline the words in this letter which refer to the writer. Then rewrite the letter with the You Attitude.

The You Attitude

Dear Mr. Winfield:

   We are in receipt of your letter requesting permission to franchise our product in Utah. We always appreciate receiving a letter from agents who wish to handle our soap. We have received more submissions than we can easily handle.

   In any case, I am afraid that it is against our policy to sell distributor rights to more than one franchisee in cities of less than 7,000, and as Mr. Hicraft is already open for business in Crow Creek, I regret we cannot authorize another agency.

   If we decide to change our marketing policy we will contact you. We will keep your name on file for six months.

                                        Sincerely,
                                        Derek Jones

   This letter does not display the You Attitude. All the underlined words refer to Mr. Jones and *his* company.

   Rewritten from the You Attitude point of view, the letter might come out like this:

Dear Mr. Winfield,

   Thank you very much for your interest in becoming a franchisee for Super Soap Systems. Your application was most welcome.

   In order to protect our franchisees, our policy is to award one franchise in cities with a population of less than 7,000. As you may know, Mr. Winfield, Mr. Hicraft currently has the rights to the Crow Creek franchise.

However, if you would care to apply for the
franchise in Elbow Grease, your application would
receive immediate favorable attention. Please let me
know if you find this alternative acceptable.

Sincerely,
Derek Jones

EXERCISE 8

The underlined words create a negative tone in
the following memo. Only one word can be
circled as positive.

*Identifying
Negative
Words*

Some couriers have carelessly sent all their
undelivered parcels on to the Halifax depot for
storage. This has created several problems.

Therefore, supervisors should eradicate any
worthless parcels before forwarding them. The
Halifax depot suffers from the general space
problems too. We are not a garbage dump.

Do not hesitate to submit further difficulties to this
office for the inclusion in our list of problem areas
within the organization.

To calculate the negative/positive word ratio
here:

Tone
Evaluation

1 Multiply the negative words × 5:
  11 × 5 = 55
1 Multiply the positive words × 1:
  1 × 1 = 1

Tone
Interpretation

Conclusion: The 55:1 negative/positive
word ratio indicates that the letter
possesses an extremely poor tone.

3 ORGANIZING YOUR REPORTS

OBJECTIVES:

- Write an Acceptable Core Sentence

- Create a Detailed Outline

- Write Effective Cue Cards

- Write a Well-Organized Short Report

- Use Graphics Effectively

INTRODUCTION: THE McKEOWN METHOD

In Section 1, you learned how to organize a *power sentence*, and in Section 2 you learned how to organize the psychological and physical layout of your letters. Section 3 will introduce you to the "McKeown Method" of organizing larger-scale writing projects, such as procedures manuals and reports.

The McKeown Method of writing reports consists of six main steps:

1 Constructing the Core Sentence
2 Writing the Outline
3 Collecting Information on Cue Cards
4 Writing your First Draft without Pausing
5 Performing a Final Edit of the Text
6 Inserting Appropriate Graphics.

The McKeown Method's unique six-step approach to report writing depends upon constructing a perfect plan *before* collecting data. The method will cut your report writing time dramatically, and ensure that you turn out *perfectly organized* reports—which are seen as rarely as roses in snow.

Reports range in length from a two-page accident report, to a ten-page financial report, to a two-thousand-page analytical report. Each type calls for a different emphasis. If you want comprehensive, detailed information about how to write a particular kind of report, there are a number of other handbooks that you can turn to, such as Ingrid Brunner's *The Technician as Writer: Preparing Technical Reports* (Indianapolis: Bobbs-Merrill, 1983).

Despite their differing lengths, however, all reports require *clear organization.* Finding the right order for an immense amount of data provides the central challenge in most reports. The art of efficient report writing demands the use of a "systems approach" to achieve this organized quality consistently. This section provides instruction and exercises to help you begin to *master* such an approach individually.

WHAT IS A REPORT?

A report is a written communication sent from someone who has acquired information to someone who wants to use that information. In addition, it has these three characteristics:

1 Considerable research
2 Greater complexity and detail in the letter or memorandum
3 Meticulous organization.

Of central significance, a finished report presents the *results* of investigation and research. Contrary to popular belief, it does *not* explore—it presents the *results* of an exploration. Of course, writers of reports do not know their exact destination when they begin thinking about a project. However, by the time they begin to **write** their report they must know *exactly* where they will finish. By separating the idea of research from the idea of writing, we remove all excuses for sloppy organization of written work: when you have **completed** your research, and know the answer to a question, you can organize your writing to lead your reader to the same conclusion clearly.

The McKeown Method uses a systems approach to writing organized reports. An analogy with the growth of a tree may help you to understand the relationship between each of the three preliminary steps in writing a report.

Like the trunk of a tree, the *core sentence* is of primary importance, since its shape provides the main supporting structure for the report. The *outline*, like the major branches of the tree, comes next, determining the direction and the extent of the coverage in the report. Finally, the *cue cards* contain the individual facts clustered under the generalized outline, resembling individual leaves clustered on the tree's main branches.

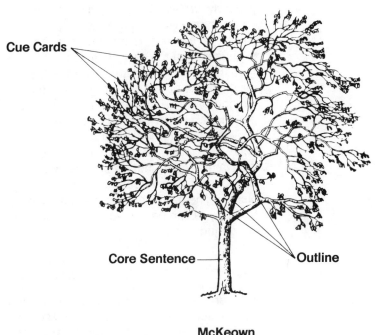

Cue Cards

Core Sentence

Outline

**McKeown
Method**

Once these three stages have been completed, the report's organization is set as if in concrete; the remaining three stages — writing, editing and inserting graphics — follow quickly and easily. Because the up-front work decides the organizational quality of the finished report, it deserves your most careful attention.

I *THE CORE SENTENCE*

A *DESCRIPTION*

As a first step in writing any report, the McKeown Method requires a core sentence. If properly written, this sentence ensures that your report will accomplish exactly what you want it to, and not wander off track. The significance of the core sentence lies in the fact that every good report expresses a single major theme or focus. This central intention can therefore be expressed in a single "one-main-idea" sentence. The core sentence provides a patterned structure to assure that you have clearly defined your focus, or final goal in the report, before beginning, much as you focus a camera carefully *before* taking a picture. The more care you take, the more certain you can be that your picture will be sharp and clear.

STRUCTURE OF THE CORE SENTENCE

The core sentence presents certain types of information in each of six carefully sequenced "compartments." These six compartments follow an *invariable* order:

1 The subject
2 The verb
3 The object
4 The linking phrase
5 A numeral
6 The names of the major divisions of the report, in the order in which they will appear in the text.

Here is an example of a core sentence:

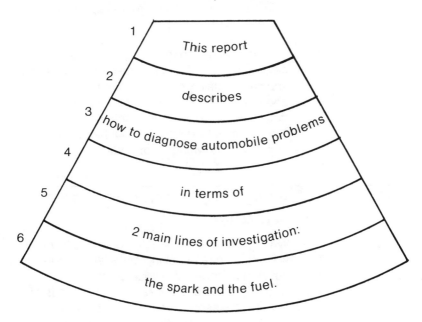

The numbers in the above example correspond to the following components within the core sentence:

1 The *grammatical* subject: "This report."
2 A specific action verb in the present tense: e.g., "lists, compares, contrasts, describes" [not verb phrases like "is about," or "deals with," which are too vague].
3 An object-noun, or noun-phrase, describing the general topic of the report: "how to diagnose automobile problems."
4 A linking phrase (e.g., "in terms of," "with regard to," "composed of").
5 A number. (Usually the number 2 or 3— sometimes 4, 5 or 6) standing for the number of major divisions covered by the report. Ninety percent of all reports have either two or three major divisions.

6 The names of the major components (listed in the order in which they will appear as sections of the report).

It may seem odd to write this core sentence before you have done any research. However, you can relatively quickly find out enough about the topic of your planned research to decide what major components must be covered in your report, without being sucked down into the whirlpool of details.

BENEFITS OF THE CORE SENTENCE APPROACH

Writing a core sentence prevents you from wasting time researching material you will never incorporate into your report. Understanding this will save you hundreds of hours of research, and is the most valuable lesson you can ever learn about writing reports. Remember, the core sentence is designed to guide you, not your reader. It focuses your attention on the bull's eye of the target you are shooting at: your report's central idea.

Because of its predominant importance, be sure to write the core sentence for every report exactly in the recommended form. If you omit any one of the six categories, or change its order, or add anything, you depart from the system's approach. The core sentence must be clinically sparse, with no extra words to fog your meaning. It avoids persuasive, advertising language; it shuns humor and ornament. It puts your thinking exactly on target, so you reach your destination (the completed report) as quickly as possible. Yes, this makes for a predictable and boring sentence structure, but it also ensures consistency of results—and these results will be excellent.

Oddly enough, the core sentence must be difficult to write if it is to be valuable. This is because the hardest decision in writing any report is how to organize the material, and what material to include. Your core sentence must solve these problems before you go further. If you find it easy to write, it is not likely to be useful. You should spend 25 percent of the time allotted to writing the report simply writing this one sentence—so experiment until you get it right.

EXERCISE 12

Write a core sentence for a report describing everything that you have done today. Begin with the subject, "This report." Continue with the verb, "describes." You will soon notice that you can divide the day, and therefore your report, according to a number of different categories: by time, by event, by location. Choosing the most appropriate category poses the central problem in writing every report and essay. Try writing a different core sentence for each category. Then compare them and choose the best. Go through this selection process thoughtfully and carefully. Do not fall in love with your first choice. Almost always, your second or third versions will be more profound and useful.

Writing a Core Sentence I

B OTHER USES FOR THE CORE SENTENCE

Although the core sentence works well with long, complex reports, you can also use it for other jobs. For example, you can use it to define what you mean to say in a memo. Simply begin, "This memo lists safety hazards on the plant floor in terms of 4 contributing causes: . . ." Also, you can use it to predetermine what you intend to say in a letter: "This letter answers the concern about chemical spills in terms of three safety measures: . . ." Similarly, use it to plan a schedule: "This plan divides marketing sales targets into three time categories: pre-production, production, post-production." The core sentence uses analysis to solve problems: your imagination can apply it to help solve any analytical task.

EXERCISE 13

Buy a package of hard candy and examine it carefully (no eating yet!). You are about to write a report that describes the name, packaging and contents of this product to someone who has never seen a package of hard candy. Though this task may seem trivial, it is not; it calls for the same skills needed for any sort of report: careful observation and the willingness to attend to details—so do your best. (Alternatively, write a report *on a topic of your choice*.)

Writing a Core Sentence II

Write a core sentence for your report. Divide the six sections of your core sentence with strokes of your pen, and number each section to make sure you have included all six. Check your answer against the answer key on page 124.

II   *THE OUTLINE*

A   *DESCRIPTION*

After writing the core sentence, you create an outline. The outline takes up a single sheet of 8½″ × 11″ paper, and consists of headings and subheadings which briefly indicate the topic to be written about at each successive stage of the report. For an example of an outline, see page 108.

PURPOSE OF THE OUTLINE

The outline provides an economical guide for your thought and your research. Like the core sentence, it primarily serves the writer of the report—*not* the reader. Its left-brain function is to *order* thought throughout the report in a logical and natural way. Any detour in your thinking can be spotted in the outline, *before* you write, rather than *after* you finish the report.

PAGE LAYOUT FOR THE OUTLINE

This section demonstrates the kind of outline most commonly used. Notice that the major headings use all capital letters, while the subheadings use only initial capital letters; notice too that the left margin of the subheading is indented (by 5 spaces on a typewriter) from that of the major headings. This consistent patterning allows quick spotting of inconsistencies. For example, each heading or subheading must have a partner: you cannot usefully divide a section into a single

subsection, since this would not indicate the
split of a generalized section into smaller units.
Also, such a formalized layout makes it easy to
compare headings of the same importance,
since they all will have the same left margin. If
they exhibit parallelism, they will likely have
divided the major section into logical sub-units.
Such inconsistencies indicate insufficient
planning, and provide flashing orange warning
lights that can prevent later disaster at the
writing stage.

SAMPLE OUTLINE

LIMITATIONS OF THE OUTLINE

When splitting major headings, subheadings,
and sub-subheadings, it is important to know
when to stop. In general, even the smallest
level of heading indicates that three to six facts
can be grouped under it—just as three to six
staff members report to even the lowest level

of management. When writing an outline for one- or two-page reports, you may wish to include single facts as headings, but this is not the way to handle longer reports. In practice, you keep splitting categories until you find you have gone far enough for your purpose—then you back up, erasing headings until you find a level at which the heading incorporates the required three to six facts.

B *OTHER USES FOR THE OUTLINE*

MANAGER'S PRE-APPROVAL

The major additional advantage to the outline is that it allows you to gain approval for the extent and coverage of your report before writing it. If your manager approves the purpose of the report as indicated in the core sentence, likes the names and order of the major divisions of the report as they appear in the outline, and approves the sequence of small details as they appear in the sub-headings of the report, then you can write the report in full confidence that its final structure will be approved without revision. Simply obtain your manager's initialled approval of the draft outline of your report. If changes are required, they should be made then—saving you hours writing a report that will not be approved because it is off-topic, and saving your manager countless hours waiting to see your overall approach.

OTHER BENEFITS OF THE OUTLINE

The outline can be used for three other purposes. First, you can use it to write the agenda for meetings—gaining pre-approval in the way mentioned above. Second, you can use it to structure in-class essay questions. In this case, you do not use cue cards because of time pressure, but the outline will structure your essay—setting it far above most others. Third, you can use it to structure essays for outside courses at a college or university, as in business management courses. It works like a charm.

EXERCISE 14

Preparing an Outline

Generate two different possible outlines for the report described by your core sentence in Exercise 13. Include major headings, sub-headings, and sub-subheadings. Look carefully at the candy, using all five senses in your analysis, and practice being *specific*. Do not overlook even the smallest detail. Then choose the best outline of the two, and check it against the one given in the answer key on page 125.

III CUE CARDS

A DESCRIPTION

Cue cards are 3″ × 5″ index cards on which you collect your factual information, guided by your outline. They normally relate only one fact. In practice, this means from one to three sentences. Under no circumstances write on the back of the card, for this slows the final ordering.

Example of a Cue Card

> II A 1: Number and shape
>
> The package contains twelve candies. Each is circular in shape, one-quarter inch in diameter, and one-eighth of an inch thick.

Read over your compositions and, when you meet a passage which you think is particularly fine, strike it out.
—Samuel Johnson

NOTE: The cue card is cross-referenced to the outline (given in the answer key) in the upper left corner.

Leave blank space on the card surrounding the idea; this "negative space" acts like the frame on an oil painting, isolating it for observation and criticism. If every individual fact passes this scrutiny, your report will be reliable in every detail.

The most tedious part of writing a report is compiling the cue cards, so restrict their use to longer reports (over four pages in length) where you cannot expect to hold large numbers of facts in your head for long periods of time. Use 3″ × 5″ cards rather than cut pieces of paper, for the latter tend to blow away in any office wind, cannot be stored in card boxes as easily, and will fray under the pressure of constant reference.

B   *OTHER USES FOR CUE CARDS*

VERBAL REPORTS

Cue cards help create order if you are recording a report or seminar presentation that your secretary will translate into type. They also provide excellent reference when giving a short verbal report to small or large groups. Combining their use with right-brain techniques, you can use images instead of words on your cards—as Mark Twain did when lecturing.

UPDATING REPORTS

If you expect to update a report annually, as is the case with performance reports or quality control reports, you will find that your previous year's file of cue cards can be re-used, with only minimal updating. In essence, your file provides an individualized encyclopaedia that will grow in usefulness as it grows in size. The principle is the same as that of using stock phrases stored on a word processor, except that the phrases express your individual personality and match your own needs.

EXERCISE 15

Using the outline in Exercise 14 as your guide, assemble at least twenty cue cards for a report. Include *every possible detail*, even if it seems totally irrelevant. It is much easier to exclude data later than to remember it at the writing stage if it isn't immediately available.

Put your cue cards in final order, adding and subtracting facts as needed. *Include* cards providing transition markers, and cards for your introduction and conclusion. Pre-edit your power sentences and power paragraphs, putting them into final shape.

Assembling Cue Cards

The Bank Withdrawal Experience: Cue Card Reference

IV NON-STOP WRITING

The major problem with the writing stage occurs when, after writing the first paragraph, you go back to revise—and three hours later are still perfecting the paragraph. This is the stage where you lose the most time. Consequently, get in the habit of using the non-stop method of writing. The more difficult you find it, the more you will probably benefit. Attempt to reach that harmonious flow of ideas that provides coherence and personality to writing. Here the labor of compiling cue cards repays itself many times over. If you have completed them correctly, you will experience a sense of complete confidence and elation—a total right-brain state of awareness. Throw the cards off your desk as you write (make sure they're cross-referenced to your outline!) and enjoy the process.

Remember, too, that your practice in writing power sentences and power paragraphs in Section 1 will serve you well here. Keep to the active voice, use direct and specific words, and strive to make each sentence follow logically from the previous one.

EXERCISE 16

Writing Non-stop

Using the non-stop method, write the first draft of your report from the cue cards assembled in Exercise 15, in ten minutes or less. Revise nothing: leave all blemishes, misspellings, passive constructions, etc.

V *EDITING*

A *EDITING FOR GRAMMAR*

Make a quick check for clear sentences, specific language and correct spelling. Of course, if you pre-edited your cue cards perfectly, this check will reveal no flaws, except in the case of those transitional markers and phrases that link paragraphs.

B *CHECK YOUR CONCLUSIONS*

Read the entire report, and then check to ensure that the introduction and conclusions relate clearly to the body of the report. Remember that conclusions sum up the facts contained in the report, while recommendations provide your ideas for acting on the total *meaning* of the report. The more solid the facts in your report, the more favorably your readers will look on your recommendations.

C *INCORPORATING VISUALS*

Where possible, put graphs and charts next to the text they illustrate. If the visual takes up one-fourth of the page or less, consider placing it within the body of the written page. If it is a page in size, put it immediately after the first page of prose referring to it. Put visuals in the appendix *only* if they are merely back-up material, and not useful in clarifying or simplifying information.

You can use a number of different visual components to add style and readability to

reports: tables, line charts, bar charts
(horizontal and vertical), pie charts, flow charts,
schematic diagrams and pictograms.

TABLES

Tables save time by presenting large blocks of
quantitative information in rows and columns,
without the connecting threads of prose.
Notice that the side captions and figures read
sideways to the information in the rows to their
right. The headings, however, direct attention
to the information in all the lines directly below.

	Eastern		Central		Northern	
	A	M	S	R	B	S
1980	173	29	275	55	343	101
1982	213	45	412	110	657	233
1984	408	101	906	250	1303	504
1986	988	302	2191	698	2988	1337
1988	1213	409	2527	778	4102	1498
1990	1441	562	2829	912	5769	1603

*Table: Canceled check returns (in thousands) by region
and area*

LINE CHARTS

Use line charts to plot trends or relationships over time, on an arithmetical grid. Plot time on the horizontal axis (x-axis); plot the values of the series on the vertical axis (y-axis).

Take care not to distort the relative proportions of the horizontal and vertical scales. Obviously, by expanding one scale and contracting the other, you can convey incorrect impressions. For example, data plotted on a line chart with time intervals one-sixteenth of an inch apart will show more violent fluctuations than the same data plotted on a chart with intervals half an inch apart. Also, be careful not to rely solely on color to distinguish two lines if your report will be duplicated numerous times—use dashes or dots to individualize lines as well.

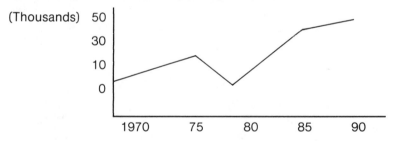

Number of internal reports released since 1970

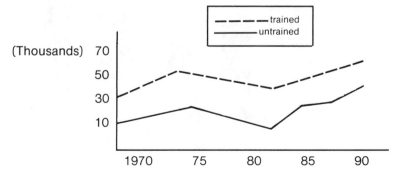

Number of internal reports written since 1970 by trained and untrained writers

BAR CHARTS

Use horizontal bars to indicate quantities of time, length or distance. Use vertical bar charts to report numbers, heights or depths.

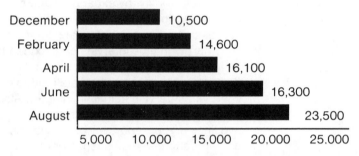

Anticipated Monthly Gross Apex Engineering: First Year of Operation

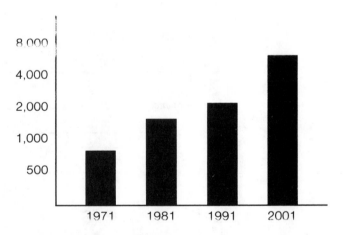

Past and Projected Numbers of On-Line Systems

PIE CHARTS

Pie charts show segments as slices sized according to the percentages of the whole: all parts combined make up 100%. Begin at 12 o'clock with the largest sector, and subdivide the circle progressively into smaller parts, moving clockwise. Do not use the pie chart for more than six items, because it becomes too difficult to read easily.

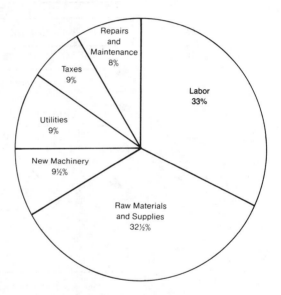

PIE CHART, *Operating Costs Breakdown, New Administrative Centre*

FLOW CHARTS

The flow chart simply indicates movement
through time. Rectangles denote actions;
diamonds indicate decisions.

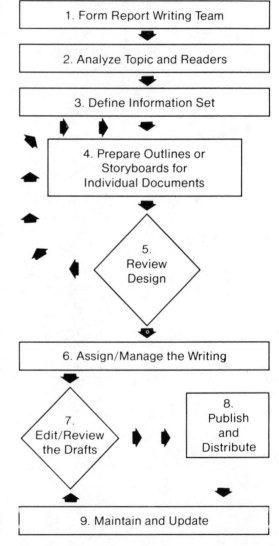

Process of Report Preparation

PICTOGRAMS AND SCHEMATIC DIAGRAMS

Clearly label and caption pictograms and schematic diagrams for maximum usefulness. Put them as close as possible to the text they illustrate, and strive for simplicity.

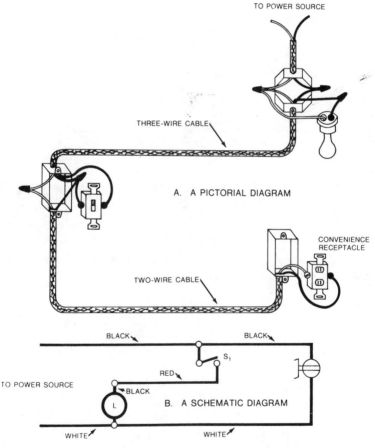

Fig. 10-5: A single-pole switch controlling a lamp with a convenience outlet powered, at all times, independently of the switch. This circuit illustrates a method of adding a switch and a convenience outlet beyond a lamp. The power enters the circuit at the lamp with the switch controlling the lamp. The power for the convenience outlet runs directly to the outlet and is independent of the switch.

PICTOGRAMS

Use pictograms to illustrate numerical
relationships in an easy-to-understand format.

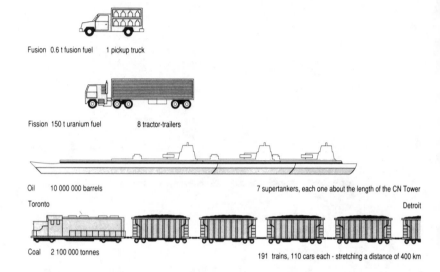

Fusion 0.6 t fusion fuel   1 pickup truck

Fission 150 t uranium fuel   8 tractor-trailers

Oil   10 000 000 barrels   7 supertankers, each one about the length of the CN Tower

Toronto   Detroit

Coal   2 100 000 tonnes   191 trains, 110 cars each - stretching a distance of 400 km

*Pictogram showing relative annual fuel requirements for a typical
1,000-megawatt power plant.*

VI SECTION SUMMARY

This description of a "systems approach" to organizing and writing reports has given you the basic pattern. It remains to put it to work. The exercises discussed will help you focus on method rather than on detail. If you have worked hard, you should with practice be able to write reports in less than half the time they used to take. Also, their organization should be much better.

Good luck!

VII *ANSWER KEY*

EXERCISE 13

*Writing a
Core
Sentence II*

Buy a package of hard candy and examine it carefully (no eating yet!). You are about to write a report that describes the name, packaging and contents of this product to someone who had never seen a package of hard candy. Though this task may seem trivial, it is not; it calls for the same skills needed for any sort of report: careful observation and the willingness to attend to details—so do your best. (Alternatively, write a report *on a topic of your choice.*)

Write a core sentence for your report. Divide the six sections of your core sentence with strokes of your pen, and number each section to make sure you have included all six.

Here is one suggested version:

1	This report
2	describes
3	hard candy
4	in terms of
5	two major components:
6	packaging and contents.

EXERCISE 14

*Preparing an
Outline*

Generate two different possible outlines for the report described by your core sentence in Exercise 13. Include major headings, subheadings and sub-subheadings. Look carefully at the candy, using all five senses in your analysis, and practice being *specific.* Do not overlook even the smallest detail. Then choose the best outline of the two.

Here is one suggested outline:

I. PACKAGING
   A. Outer Wrapper
      1. Name
      2. Appearance
      3. Material
   B. Inner Wrappers
      1. Wax
      2. Foil
II. CONTENTS
   A. Appearance
      1. Number and shape
      2. Colors
   B. Smell/Taste/Texture

Notes:
   1. This is only one of many possible outlines. Have you produced an equally effective one? If your outline is less detailed, review the instructions and notice the critical importance of going into sufficient detail. The greater number of sub-categories you create, the better organized your report.
   2. *Do not* begin to write your report if you cannot think your way through to the smallest level of detail on the outline. Without forcing yourself to this level of specificity, you will find that the systems approach will fall apart—and your report will ramble.

INDEX